"THE POINT"

of

Newport, RI

Eileen G. Nimmo

In collaboration with John L. Nimmo

This book is Number 348
of a limited edition
of 1000.

Published by
J & E Publishing
99 Third Street, Suite 201
Newport, RI 02840

Printed by
King Printing Company
181 Industrial Ave., East
Lowell, MA 01852

Cover photo: The Hunter House, 54 Washington St., Newport, R.I.
Owned by the Preservation Society of Newport County.

Cover and graphic design, digital photography and scanning by Dona Walkup

Traditional photography by Jeff Brown

Library of Congress Control Number: 2001126425

International Standard Book Number (ISBN): 0-9710040-0-5

Dedicated to my husband

William Nimmo, Jr.

who urged me to write this book.

He helped me in so many ways but did not live to see the finished work. I dedicate this book to him with all my love.

****

We walked these streets hand in hand
Together, you and I.
But one must go and one must stay
I cannot question why.

When flowers bloom and the sun sets low,
When leaves turn brown and fall,
I walk again down Memory Lane
And hear you softly call.

Winter nights ... snow is falling,
The wind is blowing across the bay.
I hear your laughter. I see your smile.
You are never far away.

Time will dull the heartache and
Time will let me see
That all things have a reason.
Such things are meant to be.

Table of Contents

Houses

Houses - continued

Acknowledgements

Writing a book is a long undertaking. It has been nine years since I sat at a table in Squaw Valley, California, the snow past the roof tops, house bound for fourteen days. It was then that an old fashioned typewriter was placed before me and my husband and niece said, "Write a book about the Point" and so this book was born.

My parents taught me a respect for education. I have always yearned to seek further knowledge. Writing this book has been a wonderful experience; pursuing the history of the lives of the people I have written about has been fascinating. They have come alive as I have researched their history. I have felt as though I lived it with them.

I can say I have enjoyed the time spent on this book. It has also helped me to deal with changes in my own life. However, there are those to whom I owe a great deal of gratitude and without whom I could never have completed the task. To them I owe more than mere words could describe.

To my husband Bill, who died when the book was halfway completed. He was born on the Point and loved it as only a "Point Hummer" can. He participated in the stories with me, making comments and suggestions all along the way. How he would have loved to see the finished product

To my niece Rebecca Hayes-Andrews, who first suggested the book. It was with her constant encouragement and persistence that I found the courage and determination to forge ahead. This is her "brainchild". Brought up on "The Point," she transplanted to Squaw Valley, California, where she resides with her husband and two children. She insists that someday they will all return.

To my brother-in-law, John L. Nimmo, I owe so very much. He spent so much time coordinating, revising, making corrections. The book absolutely could not have been completed without his assistance. "Born On The Point" he and his family reside in Natick, Massachusetts; but his heart is here in Newport and this book means as much to him as it does to me. My gratitude to him can never be expressed.

To all of the librarians at the Redwood Library, the Newport Library, Salve Regina Library, and the Middletown Library who so graciously assisted me in searching for materials, my thanks.

To The Newport Preservation Society, The Newport Restoration Foundation, The Rhode Island Historical Society, The Newport Historical Society and The Point Association of Newport, my appreciation.

To my friends and neighbors who contributed their time, their mementos, their pictures, their stories, I can only express my gratitude.

Time has been frozen on the Point for over two hundred years. To all the people of whom I write, to those of whom I do not write, they might, if they could speak, thank those who helped preserve their lovely homes in this once great shipping port. To them I am grateful for the heritage they left. They were the beginning, the inspiration. Although dead, they are seemingly alive and perchance when you stroll through the narrow streets, you will view the homes and remember that once many years ago these people laughed, and cried, lived and loved within their walls. They are all long since gone but they will live on in our memories.

Newport Bridge as seen from the U.S. Naval Hospital grounds

Introduction

This book was written because of a love for Newport, Rhode Island, a small town of approximately 26,000 people, where families have shared their joys, tears and memories throughout the years, where friends are truly friends and memories are for a lifetime.

Many stories have been written of the Ocean Drive and Bellevue Avenue with their glittering mansions and fascinating occupants from the Astors and the Vanderbilts of the past to the Pells and vonBulows of today.

To most people Newport conjures visions of a summer playground: Bailey's Beach, The Newport Country Club, The Casino, the mansions, and the homes of the rich and the prominent. There is more to Newport. Thornton Wilder spoke of the "Nine Cities" of Newport in one of his many wonderful books, and we will write of this further in this book. While it is true that Newport is known for all of this, there are other areas of interest found in the old town that is full of memories of a former and much simpler age.

"The Point," a lovely secluded section of Newport, was chosen as our subject because it is one of the oldest sections of the city where many of the 18th century homes have been restored and also because it is my home.

It is not a large area, being bounded on the south by Long Wharf and the inner harbor, on the west by Washington Street and Narragansett Bay, to the north by the Naval Base and to east by Thames and Farewell Streets. Small though it may be, the Point is beloved by all. It is a place to walk along the waterfront, to enjoy the cool breezes, the beautiful homes, the incomparable harbor, the magnificent yachts, and to greet the other "Point Hummers" as they stroll throughout the Point, especially on Washington Street.

Wouldn't it really be something to go back in time, to be able to see and hear images from the long gone past? To be able to wander down the narrow streets, gaze at the old homes and meet and speak with people who, in every way, exhibit the manner and style of an era gone by?

Many years ago I read a story of a small boy who, while playing, picked up a strange object on the street. It was shaped much like a horseshoe. There was a word engraved on it but try as he might, the boy could not pronounce the word. He tried and tried and suddenly one day he said the word correctly and immediately the object began to grow larger in his hand. It became bigger and bigger until it was as big as a door. He stepped through the door and found himself in a strange land. We, too, can pass through that archway and travel back to another time, another century and stroll through the Point, as it was, and as it is. Its beautiful homes have many stories to tell. Our memories are one thing that can never be bought or sold. They are ours and ours alone. We can, however, share them.

We are neighbors with those who lived here in the past as well as those who live here in the present. We walk where they have walked; we live where they have lived. The Point, a place that seems frozen in time, was theirs, is now ours, and will in the future belong to others.

"Born on the Point" in Newport and never having left for any extended period, the Point and Newport will forever be part of my life and my memories

Because I love it so and before time dims my memory, I want to write of all that it was, all that it is, so that those who follow will know it too, and that those who have shared it with me will remember. I belong to Newport and, in return, Newport and all that it is belongs to me.

Prelude

All our lives we will remember these places and their special moments.
Many are gone.....many remain..... many have changed
but each one of us has special memories of family, lovers and friends
with whom we shared special moments here.
Some are living..... some are dead,
but in our hearts we have loved them all.

Easton's Point

Stroll through the narrow, crooked streets of the Point and you will find houses dating from the beginning of Newport's history. Not replicas, these are the original homes. Here ships, laden with sugar and molasses from the Indies and goods from European ports, arrived daily. Here, from their distilleries, their candle making warehouses, their furniture building shops, their silver-making shops, the Newport merchants exported their merchandise.

If you have been fortunate enough to have the Point as your birthplace, you will be given a certificate by the Point Association stating that you have been "Born on the Point." Being a resident of the Point gives you the privilege of being called a "Point Hummer"

Many have questioned, "What is a Point Hummer?" The name goes back to the time when a group of men would gather at the Elm Street driftway in the evenings and spend the twilight hours humming their favorite tunes. They never sang, they just hummed. Thus evolved the name "Point Hummer." It became a by-word. The baseball and softball leagues became known as the "Point Hummers." Questions as to where you lived were clarified by "I'm a Point Hummer."

In the 17th Century, the Point was the most prestigious part of Newport. It was then, and still is today, a wonderful place to live.

"Newport - City By The Sea"

What did you think would happen
When you landed on our shore?
Did you s'pose you could sail away
And dream of it no more?

Not so, my lads and lassies
You'll ne'er more be the same
For touching foot to Newport's soil
And hearing called her name.

For all who walk within the Point
A haunting spell is cast.
Step gently on this hallowed ground
You're treading on the Past.

By Eleanor S. Weaver

The Point extends out into the harbor, just north of the center of Newport. This is an area that was granted to Quaker proprietors who divided it into lots in the early 1700s. Here along the waterfront, in the early part of the 18th Century, these Quaker merchants built their mansions, wharves and warehouses.

It was here that vessels from all over the world were constantly loading and discharging their cargoes. Nearby were the more modest homes and the shops of the ship captains, shipwrights, and craftsmen whose lives were part of the sailing industry. Today there are approximately one hundred of these old houses on the Point, which today retains much of its earlier appearance. The oldest dwelling in Newport is the Wanton-Lyman-Hazard House on Broadway that was built in 1675. Most of the remaining houses date from the 18th Century.

Approximately eleven hundred houses were standing in Newport at the beginning of the Revolutionary War in 1776. The British destroyed four hundred houses and many others burned over the years. Today there are about four hundred houses in Newport that were built before 1840, three hundred of which possibly predate the Revolutionary War. The majority of these houses are on "The Point."

In the 1700s, the Point was the exclusive area of Newport. Here the merchant princes, the Quakers, the Jews, the Christians, the wealthy, the ship owners, and the wellborn lived in opulent tranquility side by side. The American Revolution changed this. England resented Newport's prosperity and competition. When the war became inevitable, Newport was one of the first places to be occupied. The British fleet patrolled the harbor and then the troops occupied the town itself. The Point was overrun with soldiers who were quartered in the homes regardless of the wishes of the owners. During the Revolution the town was under martial law. After three years of occupation, the British left the town in ruins and commerce was over, never to be known again as it was before.

Newport experienced many changes in the years after the Revolutionary War. Its fortunes fluctuated. The coming of Society, the Civil War, the robber barons, two world wars, the expansion of the Navy, the Torpedo Station, the loss of the Navy, and the closing of the Torpedo Station. All had tremendous effects on its citizens.

Over the years, the city had grown. The Point, as did other areas of Newport, became rundown and neglected. Separated as it was by the railroad, it became literally "the other side of the tracks."

When the Navy left Newport many of the houses were abandoned. Poor blacks or welfare clients inhabited many more. Rents were affordable. Now, with all the revitalization, everything changed. Property values soared.

The Eighteenth Century homes became very popular. People vied for their ownership. Welfare and poor families became distressed as their housing was swept out from under them. Now with all these organizations imbued with the spirit of restoration, the Point became once again the epitome of Colonial Newport and a great piece of preserved Americana. Most of these homes have been original-ly and beautifully restored, making "Easton's Point" one of the finest living examples of an authentic 18th Century neighborhood in the United States. Today, Newport is one of the few cities that retains much of its colonial heritage. The architecture of our lovely old city, built by the colonists and seafar-ers, bears a mark of culture that has been enhanced by contacts with the Old World.

Like most coastal cities, Newport has retained the secret of country living. The streets are lined with mostly wooden houses, each with its own yard or garden, small though it may be. Newport has always been blessed with a wonderful climate, changing seasons and a splendid harbor. It has had more than its share of shrewd, courageous and industrious citizens who helped make it a proud place among the colonial cities. In the narrow, quaint streets by the waterfront, the doorways of the Revolutionary and pre-Revolutionary period homes have unique and beautiful treatments. The pineapple, symbol of hospitality, adorns many homes.

Someone once said that we should not be like Lot's wife, standing forever in one spot, looking backward at something that should have been forgotten long ago, unwilling or unable to face forward and go on. One of the most valuable lessons we can learn is to turn loose something that is not worth keeping.

Colonial Newport is worth keeping. Our past is worth keeping. Remembering is necessary for growth. We must have feeling for what our past means, and for what our fathers and forefathers fought. Our memories are the one thing that can never be bought or sold. They are ours and ours alone. We may become discouraged now and then when things are not going quite right. You think about the things that happened in the past and you recall happy memories and you want to be back in that time again. Without our memories there would be emptiness, a tremendous void in our lives.

Almost too late, Newport awoke and realized that these memories and mementos of the past were being lost. "The Point" is the oldest section of the city. It is an area of beauty where residents are like an extended family with yearly picnics, bazaars, and potluck dinners. The Point Association includes not only the "Point Hummers" but also residents who now have made the Point their home and many who live elsewhere but who love the area and want to be part of the activities.

In the past thirty years, so much effort has been put into restoring this historic area that, by taking a walk on the Point to see the houses in the following sections, you can relive the 17th and 18th centuries.

There are many who still feel that "the way it was is best."

The Lonely "Sea Bird"

Actually there are two "Easton's Points" in Newport County. One is the point of land belonging to the Eastons extending into the ocean at Middletown near the public beach. The other is the "Point" of land bordering Newport Harbor that originally was the land granted to Governor Easton when the town was settled. All facts and evidence show that it is the Newport "Point" where the ship "Seabird" grounded.

In the fall of 1733, Isaac Stelle, a wealthy Newport merchant, was expecting his ship "Seabird" to make port before nightfall. On the previous day Captain Huxham, who commanded the ship, was in contact with Captain Crook who offered to tow him into the harbor when he arrived. Captain Huxham declined this offer.

Many Newporters and others gathered on the wharves to greet Captain Huxham, among them his sister. It was her son, among others, who retold the tale.

At about 2:00 P.M., a brig under full sail was sighted close to Easton's Point, plowing through rough seas and headed for Newport Harbor. She had somehow avoided "The Ledge" at the entrance to Narragansett Bay and was now too close to the Point for safety. At the last minute, the vessel suddenly changed course enough to avoid danger. It was then expected that she would drop sail and anchor in front of the town or alongside the wharf.

Then, as the fishermen and others in the area of Newport Harbor watched in amazement, she steered under full sail toward the northwest corner of the Point. No change was made in her course and no sail taken in. It was then thought that she was not bound for Newport but proceeding up Narragansett Bay. However, she was so close that those on the shore hailed her, warning her of the danger, and the need to change her course. She was heading for the beach directly north of the walls (presumably Battery Park's stone walls), but no answer was returned. It was then remarked, to the consternation of the assembled islanders, that not a man could be seen on her deck. It seemed that she was being steered by an invisible hand. After a few minutes she struck the shore within a short distance of the bewildered crowd that had hastened to the spot.

According to reports, the Seabird sailed outside and to the west of Goat Island and grounded off Ft. Greene (Battery Park) near Coasters Harbor Island, doing little damage to her hull. As she sailed in, no life could be seen aboard her, no crew, and no helmsman. When she grounded, fishermen who witnessed the entire incident boarded her. Immediately she was identified as Isaac Stelle's "Seabird," but where was Captain Huxham and his crew?

The only creatures aboard were a dog and a cat in the cabin where the stove was still warm and the kettle on. The table was set and a meal partially laid out. The captain's gown was lying at the foot of the companionway as if dropped in a hurry. The belongings of the captain and crew were undisturbed. The captain's papers were safe but the log and the longboat were missing. It was possible that during a thunderstorm the evening before the crew had panicked and thought it safer to abandon ship, taking the longboat. If so, it would be expected that traces of the longboat or bodies would be found. However, nothing was ever found of the longboat or the crew.

To this day, no one knows what invisible hand steered her safely into Newport Harbor or what possessed the crew to abandon her, if they did. Was there a mutiny, or an attempt to wreck the ship for insurance or salvage? What happened to the Captain and the crew? Why were no wreckage or bodies ever found?

Isaac Stelle had the Seabird refloated and repaired. She was sold and renamed the "Beachbird" and continued as a merchant vessel until just before the Revolution. Finally when the British occupied Newport, she was stripped down and guns were mounted on her hull.

The story of the beached ship, the missing crew, with no signs of illness, violence, or storm damage to her sails, spars or gear remains a mystery. Her story has been handed down from generation to generation by word of mouth until it has become a legend.

1. Early History

Newport is the southernmost of the three towns on Aquidneck Island. Portsmouth is the northernmost and Middletown, so named because of its location, lies between them. The first settlers were the Wampanoag Indians, who were forced northward off the island by the Narragansett Indians. The earliest recorded and documented voyage to the area was that of an Italian navigator, Giovanni da Verrazano, pictured at left, who sailed for the King of France and explored the coast of North America.

He explored from the vicinity of Cape Fear, North Carolina to the Maine coast. He anchored in Newport harbor for 15 days sometime between 1524 and 1528. On his next journey he again crossed the Atlantic, heading for South America. He never returned and it was believed that Indians in Brazil killed him.

In 1638, William Coddington broke away from the colony that Roger Williams had established for religious freedom in Providence. Joining him were Nicholas Easton, John Coggeshall, William Brenton, Tom Hazard, Henry Bull and William Dyre. Together they left Providence because they disagreed with the authorities in Boston regarding the Antinomian Movement, a religious controversy between moral law and faith. They believed that trust in God was more important than obedience to laws. This controversy brought many dissenters from Massachusetts to Rhode Island.

Roger Williams

These men, with help from Roger Williams, purchased Aquidneck Island from the Indians. They settled in the Portsmouth area of the island near the area now known as Common Fence Point. They took the name of Pocasset.

Anne Marbury Hutchinson was born about 1591 and grew up in England when it was torn apart by religious dissent. She was an outspoken clever woman, hardworking, and skilled in nursing. She was a follower of the Puritan minister, John Cotton. When King James I succeeded Queen Elizabeth I, he placed strict controls on England's churches. This infuriated dissidents and fueled the Puritan movement. John Cotton left England for the colonies. When he left for the New World, Anne, her husband, and their children followed. Anne began inviting men and women to her home where they discussed Cotton's sermons. Women had little role in either church or civic affairs at that time. However, Anne began to express her own beliefs that differed from those of the established ministry. The church and state were shocked

11

The Trial of Anne Hutchinson
Courtesy of the Newport Historical Society

at what they considered an attack on their teachings. The ministers believed that Anne was preaching sedition, disturbing the tranquility of the state, and they called her group the Antinomians, or the lawless ones.

In 1638, she and her family were banished from Massachusetts and they traveled to Portsmouth, Rhode Island where they joined a group established there. However, as time passed, some of the new emigrants led by Anne Hutchinson, began to gain political control. Hutchinson remained in Portsmouth for four years when a religious disagreement divided the settlement. By the next year William Coddington, Nicholas Easton, Dr. John Clark and other original settlers moved to the southern part of the island.

After the death of her husband William in 1643, Anne Hutchinson left the colony for Westchester County, New York. The Dutch, who were very tolerant in religious matters, controlled this territory. The Indians were bitter because of the harsh treatment by the settlers. Anne and five of her children were slaughtered on August 16, 1645, along with eleven other members of the household. One daughter Susan was taken captive, later ransomed, and returned to Rhode Island. Anne has been called "The American Jezebel."

Home of Gov. William Coddington
Courtesy of the Newport Historical Society

Newport was, for a considerable time, an outpost of civilization with only Indians as neighbors and miles of forest between it and the settlements of Massachusetts and Connecticut. Relations between the early settlers and the Indians were friendly. The Indian Sachem believed that there was enough land around the Bay for both Indians and settlers and that they could coexist in peace.

On May 16, 1639, they formally named this portion of the island "Newport." A little settlement was developed around a spring and extended southward to the ocean. The town formed along the harbor and originally consisted of Thames Street (named after the Thames River in England), Spring Street (for the spring from which the townspeople drew their water), Marlborough Street and Tanner Street. These streets ended at the Parade that is now known as Washington Square. Later house lots were laid out on the northern end of the Parade and these were approximately four acres each. The first house was built on Farewell Street for Nicholas Easton. The Indians burned this home in 1641.

Farewell Street was so named because it leads to the largest of the early burial sites. On its northern end it is bordered on both sides by cemeteries. In the small Coddington Cemetery, on its southern end, are buried the men and women who founded and governed this beautiful city.

The Northwest corner of Newport became known as Easton's Point. This land was granted to Nicholas Easton when Newport was first settled. When Nicholas died he left over sixty acres to his wife, Ann. Since all property was considered to belong to the husband, when Ann Easton married Henry Bull, it became his property and was thence known as "Bull's Point."

Henry died before his wife, so Ann got the property back. In July 1698, Ann Bull sold 65 acres of the land on Easton's Point to the Quakers. In the early 1700s, they began dividing it into lots that they sold to merchants, craftsmen and sea captains. The principal asset of this land was its accessibility to the water. It became known as "The Point" section of Newport. It was separated from Long Wharf and all its frenzied activities by a cove, which no longer exists

The naming of the streets followed a pattern that the Quaker William Penn established in Philadelphia. He did not believe in "man worship" and felt that streets should not be named in their honor. Therefore, the east-west streets of Philadelphia were named after trees. The north-south streets were named after numbers. "The Point" followed his example. However, in later years, First Street, the street on the waterfront, was renamed Water Street. At a later date it became Washington Street after George Washington's visit to the town. The residents admired him so they renamed the street in his honor.

The lots in the area were relatively small. The purchases came from men who outfitted the ships, and small tradesmen and craftsmen who found it convenient to be able to load their wares on boats moored in the cove at their back doors.

Sea captains discovered the area. They liked its tranquility and proximity to their ships. They built more spectacular homes along Washington Street. The homes we see on this street today had, at their back door at one time, gardens, warehouses, docks and all sorts of shops. It was a quiet, peaceful and busy time.

Newport's fine harbors attracted settlers of every religious persuasion. Many people who were unwelcome elsewhere came to Newport. Irish, Italian and Portuguese Catholics came to farm, to fish and to labor. The Orthodox Greeks, for many years, dominated the waterfront and opened fine restaurants.

The Jews and Quakers who had been banished and persecuted elsewhere in the world came to Newport because of its religious tolerance. They flourished here and went on to dominate the Town's economy and society in the next century. They contributed much to the town that had so hospitably received them. All these different nationalities added to the culture of the town in their own way and a lovely and a prosperous settlement developed.

2. The Seventeenth Century

Our journey through the Point begins in the last half of the 17th Century. It was back then that the Rhode Island colonists turned to sea trade that was much more profitable than farming. The harbor became the central point of industry and wealth. Ships brought cargoes of sugar, spices, molasses and slaves from the West Indies to the many wharves on the harbor. From Britain came manufactured goods.

Newport merchants bought salt from the Mediterranean, wood from Honduras, molasses from the West Indies. The molasses was distilled into rum at Newport, the rum exchanged for slaves on the coast of Africa, and finally the slaves were brought to the Caribbean and sold. With the proceeds, molasses was purchased and returned to New England again to be converted to rum.

Ironically, the purchase of slaves from Africa was legal, while the purchase of molasses from Haiti was not. Haiti was the most convenient source. In order to protect their brandy industry, the French masters of the island forbade the manufacture of rum there. The Governor decreed that in order to reach the colonies, Haitian molasses must first be shipped to France, then exported to England and then resold to the colonies. This made it a very expensive commodity. The "Triangular Trade," as it was called, reaped tremendous profits and later generations would try to disassociate themselves from the source of their great wealth.

As the 20th Century bootleggers, during Prohibition, enlarged their operations into illegal areas, the colonial shipmasters, in order to flaunt unreasonable restrictions, slipped over the line into piracy. Furniture, china and luxury goods came from England, Portugal and the Orient. They traded with France and Spain but were not above privateering against French and Spanish ships.

The houses owned by these wealthy merchants featured circular stairways, paneled walls, marble fireplaces, cornices and mahogany doors. These were beautiful houses. They were not the houses designed by Richard Morris Hunt, or the mansions whose interiors were imported piece by piece from Europe. These were the homes built by merchants called the "Quaker Grandees." Not permitted to wear grand clothes, the Quakers dressed their houses instead, displaying silver and gold in them "such as even the Queen did not own."

On Water Street, now Washington Street, the merchant princes built their gracious homes with their wharves and shops close at hand. In 1800, over 21 sea captains lived on Shipwright's Street now known as Bridge Street. The Townsends and the Goddards, magnificent cabinet makers, built their homes along the cove where they could load their finely crafted furniture onto ships for export to Charleston, South Carolina and the West Indies.

On top of many of these houses can be seen a "Widow's Walk." This is an open small porch where women watched, scanning the harbor for a ship that many times never returned. For long before the era of the clipper, Newport's ships sailed the seven seas while the women waited.

On the corner of Farewell and Coddington Streets, there once stood a house, probably destroyed by the British during the Revolution, belonging to Captain John Draper. He died at sea in 1739 leaving a wife and four daughters. All daughters married seamen and when he died three of the daughters were already widows. This home may not have had a "Widow's Walk" for they were mainly on the more elaborate homes such as the Hunter House.

Not all of the houses were on the grand scale of the Washington Street homes. Humble two-room houses with central chimneys still existed. Most of the humble houses would be colored a dull red. Around 1730, fancier houses were painted more vivid colors such as green, yellow and blue. However, at the end of the 18th Century the colors again became more subdued. The noted author Henry James described Newport's small houses as "little gray old ladies," which gave a quaint air to the town.

All of this was soon to change.

3. Slavery in Newport

Slavery is a state or condition by which certain persons are considered to be the property of other persons who are the absolute masters of their body and service. They are subject to their master's will and domination. The system is one of great antiquity and was practiced long ago among the Israelis, Assyrians, Babylonians, Chinese, Egyptians and most of the ancient peoples. In ancient Rome the slaves were either captives or debtors.

Because of the superiority of the white race in making war, and the comparative helplessness of the African blacks, it was common practice for the white man to invade the African coasts and capture black men and women during the 16th, 17th and 18th century. The Portuguese brought the first shipment of blacks to the New World in 1503, landing at Santo Domingo. The first slaves brought to America landed at Jamestown, Va. in 1619. From that time to the 19th century, the traffic in black people across the Atlantic was carried on by all the colonial powers.

Contrary to popular belief, most of the millions of slaves shipped from Africa were not members of an established slave population. They were ordinary farmers or members of their families who were suddenly deprived of their liberty by other Africans who reaped profits from what was a great demand for slaves by the Europeans.

Except for a few raiding parties that seized Africans and carried them off as slaves, most slaves were acquired through hard bargaining and a highly systematized trading process. Europeans would never have been allowed to penetrate inland and pillage and conquer. Africa was not filled with ignorant savages. Europeans set up trading stations with the permission of African rulers who, with their agents, were treated as business equals. Most transactions were done by barter.

Society in West Africa was divided into farmers, merchants, priests, laborers, craftsmen, scholars, etc. The elite ruled while the masses served and as their power increased so did the need for an army. The arrival of the Europeans in the 15th century brought the introduction of guns and gunpowder. The African's desire for guns and the European's desire for slaves went hand in hand.

Although in the beginning some slaves were taken forcibly, most of the Europeans acquired their slaves by a peaceful bargaining process. In the beginning, African slaves were taken to Portugal and other European cities to be used as domestic servants, a sign of affluence. When there was a shortage of farm laborers, Africans filled the void.

European greed fed African greed and vice versa. The rulers, who became involved in this tremendous trade, soon found themselves trapped in the situation. They were helpless to eliminate or reduce the trade. If they did not trade with the Europeans, all the European traders would bypass them. They would then lose the revenue and if they did not trade slaves for guns, they could not have guns. Without the guns, a ruler could not provide adequate defense and he himself could be captured and sold into slavery. Therefore the cycle continued.

When the Spaniards began to use slaves in their American colonies, the Dutch, French and British followed their example. The first slaves to arrive in the English colonies in America were from Africa. The slave traders bought only the finest specimens partly because they would be more valuable at the end of the voyage. Because of the dreadful conditions aboard the slave ship, the younger and healthier ones had a better chance of reaching their destination alive.

The Africans who became slaves underwent a terrible experience. After being chained together, marched to the coast where they underwent a naked inspection, they then endured the terrible conditions aboard the slave ship where they were starved and beaten to keep them docile. Food, light, ventilation and sanitation were minimal and only enough to keep the cargo alive and often not even enough for that. The maximum number of slaves was jammed into the hull and chained to prevent revolt and suicide. Over 20% died of dysentery or smallpox and their bodies were cast overboard. Those who survived were healthy and pretty much immune to disease. Therefore they were greatly in demand.

Upon arrival in America, they were purchased and faced a lifetime of bondage in an alien environment. They were stripped of their identities, given new names and taught that they were inferior. They would never again see their homeland.

If we are to go by the letter of the law, Roger Williams' descendants never did have the right to own slaves. In 1625, Rhode Island passed a law designed to prevent the buying of slaves. No one could hold either a black or white person in bondage for more than ten years. England, however, encouraged colonial slavery and Rhode Island followed the concept. This was in a state where the colonists demanded liberty for themselves, yet would deny it to others. In 1774, one third of the middle class in Newport owned one slave and many households had five or more. The more affluent had many more. In the South, however, because of the large plantations and the necessity for labor, the number of slaves owned greatly increased.

Newport was the port of entry for African slaves, sold on the waterfront to southern plantations in the 1700s and the basis for importing rum from the West Indies. In later years, it would become the home-port of whaling ships and the center of the spermaceti candle industry.

The Quakers were the first Americans to condemn slavery although many of the Quaker merchants were willing to reap the profits of the trade. Abraham Redwood's father was a sea captain. His mother, Mehatable Langford of Antigua was an heiress. Their fruit and sugar plantations in Antigua were entirely dependent on slaves. Rather than give up his slaves, Abraham Redwood left the membership of the Friends in 1775. He died in 1788. Many owners did free their slaves not because they wanted to, but they felt it was good business sense. They finally prohibited slavery among themselves in the 1770s.

The slave trade had been illegal in Rhode Island since 1787. Newport, however, attempted to revive the African traffic and did carry on for a short time. In 1804, Newport transported 3,500 black people to Charleston. In 1807, Federal law brought an end to this chapter of Newport's history. However, as years went by, America expanded its borders westward and saw the beginning of a national disagreement over the slavery question, which in time would eventually split the nation in two.

4. The Nine Cities of Newport

Newport has changed greatly since the 1770s. Summer visitors discovered Newport in 1784. The craftsmen, artists, actors, and writers enjoyed the quiet and peace and the close proximity to Providence, Boston, and New York. It was almost a century later before Society arrived. The coming of the railroad and coastal steamers made real estate in Newport extremely desirable. The city was located conveniently between New York and Boston. Society didn't take over the city itself. Rather, they established a suburb beyond the boundaries of the colonial town, leaving it as it was. Again, another century passed before those who came here with the Navy, the yachting crews or as tourists decided that this was the place where they wanted to live and made it the city it is today.

Newport is part of a small island that includes the other towns of Middletown and Portsmouth known as Aquidneck Island. Three bridges connect it to the outside world. Newport is in itself a place apart. It has little in common with the rest of the mainland. Native Newporters rarely leave the island. They have everything they desire right here. The town is designed for walking. It is the quickest and most convenient way to get around the narrow streets. Bicycles, when weather permits, which is about nine months per year, are seen everywhere. The island is fifteen miles long and three miles wide and that is the entire island. Newport, at its southern end, is a very small portion of that.

During the winter season, Newport belongs to the Newporters. However, when the summer arrives, the island belongs to the tourists. They come from everywhere. They come here because there is no other place like it. Large cruise ships from all over the world arrive in our harbor. Tour buses carry license plates from all over the United States. Artists and craftsmen come to our festivals and our art galleries. Sightseers come to gaze and walk through the magnificent mansions of the Golden Age. They drive the ten miles of the "Ocean Drive" to view more mansions and the astonishingly beautiful beaches with waves crashing in from the Atlantic Ocean.

The Newporters are friendly and willing to help but they keep their distance. Celebrities galore have visited from monarchs such as the Queen of England, Prince Andrew and Prince Edward, to presidents such as Washington, Ford, Kennedy, and Eisenhower. Yet, although they are welcomed graciously, most Newporters pay little attention and rarely go out of their way to meet or greet them. When Queen Elizabeth II visited Newport, Doris Duke was scheduled to represent the Newport Restoration Foundation at the welcoming ceremony. Just before the event, officials were notified that Miss Duke would not appear. No excuse was given. She sent a representative in her stead.

Those who come do so for many reasons. Small as it is, the city has so much to offer. For generations Newport was home to the America's Cup races. Its harbors are home to some of the finest yachts in the world. Its 18th Century homes are a treasury of knowledge for the historian, along with its unparalleled edifices of church and state. Where else can a fisherman find the finest lobsters in the world? Our music festivals bring together some of the finest musicians known. Our nationally known Tennis Hall of Fame was here when society was at its peak. This was the Gilded Age, when money flowed like water, when extravagance knew no bounds and a summer address in Newport was second to none. Vacationers and tourists love its incomparable ocean view and soft summer climate. Here and here alone there is something for everyone. Over a half million visitors arrive each year. They come for many reasons and many never leave.

Thornton Wilder in his book "Theophilus North" fell in love with the city. When he first arrived here, society was in full swing. He identified the following nine cities in the tiny community.

The First City he felt belonged to the early settlers and revolved around what we call "The Old Stone Mill" on Bellevue Avenue. Visualize, if you will, this round tower standing as it does at the top of Historic Hill. Think back to the days when there were no houses around it, just rolling land down to the waterfront. Was it a mill built by the ancestors of Benedict Arnold? Was it a relic of the Vikings who once landed here, or did it have another significance to those people who built it? To this date, no one has the answer. It was there when the colonists were here. Did they have the answer?

The Second City is the town itself. It holds some of the most beautiful and elegant private edifices in America. The town played a dramatic part in the War of Independence. Torn asunder by the destructive forces of England, the town rallied with support from the French forces and launched a sea campaign that successfully turned the course of the war.

The Third City was the west side of Thames Street. It once contained the wharves of New England's most prosperous seaport. Here were the docks and chandlers and the establishments where one glimpsed drying nets and sails. Here prosperous merchants traded. The seafarers frequented the bars and taverns, which were dirty and treacherous, where no landlubber dared to venture.

The Fourth City belongs to the Army and Navy. There have always been forts defending Narragansett Bay. The Naval Training Station had expanded so much during World War II that it became a city in itself.

The Fifth City was the domain of a number of highly intellectual families who came from New York, Cambridge and Providence and discovered the advantages and beauty of Newport as a summer resort. Professors, writers, and philosophers all gathered here. Julia Ward Howe, the author of "The Battle Hymn of the Republic" lived and died here in her 92nd year. Stories by Edith Wharton and Henry James were written depicting scenes among the houses of the Cliff Walk. Longfellow and Poe were visitors. Many movies have been made on the lawns, in the mansions, in the center of the city, and on the Naval base aboard the ship "Constellation" that is now in Baltimore, MD. This was the city of the intellectuals who resented the intrusion of the sixth city.

The Sixth City consisted of the wealthy, the empire builders, the railroad magnets, and the robber barons who suddenly awakened to the realization that New York is crushingly hot in the summer. The cool breezes of the bay lured them. They left their castles and villas and came to Newport. They brought their wealth and fashion and became another city known as "Newport's 400."

Henry James, pictured on the next page, after a long expatriation from America, could only deplore what three decades of too much money had done to the Newport he loved. He called the mansions "white elephants." He pitied the husbands who virtually worked themselves to mental breakdowns or death in the pursuit of still more money. Their women spent their lives in idle pleasure only to succumb in their later years to various forms of insanity. The elegant idlers, the lounge lizards, the gigolos, and the permanent guests drifted from house to house.

Henry James

<u>The Seventh City</u> is that of the servants, those who never enter the front door of the mansion in which they live, except to wash it. Still, they are conscious of their closeness to the rich, their indispensability, and they band together. They develop an underground solidarity, depend upon each other, socialize together, join the same churches, and form a family of their own. They keep strictly to themselves.

<u>The Eighth City</u> This population depends upon the existence of the 5th and 6th cities. It contains the camp followers, prying journalists, parasites, the fortune hunters, the crashers, those seeking social prominence, seers, healers, protégés and protégées and private detectives.

Finally there is **<u>The Ninth City</u>**. This is the steady population. It consists of the people who will buy and sell property, raise and educate their children, bury their dead and go on with life, paying little attention to the other eight cities so close to them.

Newport is many things to many people. To the Newporters, born and bred or newly settled here, it is a home that few would trade for anywhere else.

5. The Craftsmen

The colonial local cabinetmakers were the finest of their time. They not only furnished the houses of wealthy Newporters, but their work appeared in the great homes all along the moneyed eastern shore of the Atlantic to the south.

For almost a century, between 1740 and 1840, there were about twenty craftsmen who were known as the Townsend-Goddard dynasty of cabinetmakers. These families were related both by marriage and by their Quaker faith. Their furniture, constructed first of walnut and later of mahogany, made Rhode Island famous. The identifying characteristics of the work of these artisans were the block front and the shell designs that they used on most of their creations. They produced hall clocks, desks, chests of drawers, secretaries, chairs and tables, many of which are now displayed in museums.

Rhode Island antique furniture, especially the furniture built by these craftsmen, fetches premium prices today. A desk at a recent sale brought over a million dollars in the town of Bristol. The money was used to restore the Colt mansion that once housed the desk. On June 18, 1998, Christie's Auction House sold a Townsend Chippendale chest for 4.73 million dollars. John Townsend would have been amazed that his block-and-shell desk, that he finished in 1792, fetched so much money.

Christopher Townsend's mahogany slant-type desk that he built in 1745, two hundred and fifty years later, brought the second highest price ever paid for a piece of American furniture anywhere in the world. It sold for 8.25 million dollars.

These prices were small in comparison to the final bid fetched at the auction of a desk in the home of Nicholas Brown, the Nightingale House, in Providence. The desk sold for 11 million dollars, a record price for a work of art other than a painting. The money financed the renovation of the residence, the largest surviving wooden house in America, which had suffered serious neglect and termite damage. A copy of the desk is now on display in the residence that has been turned into a museum.

According to a newspaper article dated December 25, 1992, Mrs. George Connal-Rowan of Stirling, Scotland gave a very valuable collection of Townsend-Goddard furniture to the Rhode Island School of Design (RISD) Museum and the Preservation Society of Newport County. She and her niece, Miss Muriel Case, felt that this was where the collection should go. Miss Case was the first person to privately restore one of the old colonial homes in Newport.

Silverware of that period is now a collector's item. During the early part of the 18th Century, the wealth of the Newport merchants supported the many silversmiths who worked here, among them were Samuel Vernon, Tom Arnold, Isaac Anthony, and Benjamin Brenton.

Many of the beautiful articles crafted here found their way to other parts of the world. These were believed to have been taken as mementos or souvenirs by the English and French soldiers and sailors who served in Newport during the Revolutionary War and by the Loyalists who, when leaving Rhode Island, had to leave their furniture behind but took their silver back to England with them. Several silver pieces from Rhode Island have appeared in France and Britain.

Cornelius C. Moore, a well-known Newport attorney born in Newport in 1885, was the owner of an outstanding collection of American silver as well as furniture and paintings crafted by Newport artisans. His career encompassed many phases. He was involved with the banking and educational institutions and his name was a familiar one to all Newporters. Most knew him personally. When he died in Newport in 1970, his estate stipulated that the sale of his collection of Early American silver be auctioned by Sotheby's. The proceeds of this auction were to be given to Providence College, his alma mater. He lived, not in a mansion, but a very lovely home that stood close by the famed "Old Stone Mill." His law office, on Bellevue Avenue, was just across the street.

Over the years most people have cherished their family silver, as they have no other type of possession. It has been reverently passed down through time to the next generation or to a dearly beloved friend or relative. Tea sets, candlesticks, strainers, bowls, pitchers, spoons, porringer bowls, ladles, pepper boxes, tankards, tongs, creamer and sugar bowls, all bear a touch mark which identifies the work of a particular craftsman.

When silver was given as a gift, it was usually engraved. Christening cups or spoons usually bore the initials of the child and the date of birth. Silver usually represented the wealth of the family.

6. The Revolutionary War

For more than a hundred years the town had prospered in peace and plenty, until mutterings of rebellion were heard. The first act of open rebellion against England occurred in Newport in 1769. The British ship "Liberty" was taken and scuttled in revenge for outrages perpetrated upon the citizens by her officers and crew. In 1772, another outbreak occurred when the citizens, in retaliation for British oppression, went out in boats and attacked the King's ship, "The Gaspee." They burned her and wounded her command.

The Burning of the Gaspee
Courtesy of the R.I. Historical Society

The attack resulted in the first bloodshed in the American war for liberty and was the first armed resistance by the colonists to the British Navy. The town furnished four thousand men to help man the ships of the new American Navy, from the battle of Lexington until the surrender at Yorktown.

What caused the American Revolution? Great Britain believed that the colonies should be run primarily for the benefit of the mother country. For the first century and a half the American colonies were too weak to protest effectively against this policy. They needed Britain for protection against the Indians and enemies such as France and Spain. Then too, Americans enjoyed certain economical advantages within the British imperial system. By 1763 the situation was changing. Now, well populated and prosperous, the colonies no longer needed to rely on the mother country. Rather, they felt that they could handle their own affairs efficiently and that, except in times of crisis, the English government should interfere as little as possible in colonial affairs.

Trouble began after the French and Indian War (1754-1763). Because of the British victory in that conflict, the colonial self-confidence increased for they no longer needed England's assistance along the frontier. However, the end of the hostilities enabled Britain to devote more attention to colonial affairs, to assert authority over the colony, and to try to tap colonial sources of revenue in order to pay off the war debt.

The Paper Money Act of 1764 prohibited the colonies from issuing paper currency. A tax was established on sugar and molasses brought into the colonies. The Stamp Act was established which taxed the colonies for newspapers, periodicals, marriage licenses and legal documents. Lawyers, journalists, merchants and landowners flatly refused to buy the hated stamps and boycotted British goods. Feelings mounted and finally England backed down.

However, tea was the most important beverage in the colonies. The British Tea Act of 1773 was designed to help the British East India Company, which at that time had a large tea surplus. They were once given a special tax exemption so that the Americans were able to purchase tea more cheaply than before. However, it would now be processed under special agents and the colonial dealers would suffer. On December 16, 1773, the citizens of Massachusetts disguised as Indians, dumped East India Company tea into Boston Harbor. This became known as "The Boston Tea Party."

The war for American independence was really three conflicts rolled into one. It was a fight between the thirteen colonies and Great Britain revolving around the colonial resistance to British legislation. It was also a fight within the colonies because many Americans sided with the mother country (Loyalists or Tories) against the Revolutionary Patriots (Whigs). Then, thirdly, the Revolution was part of the colonial wars between England and France.

Had the Americans been united against Britain, their task would still have been a major one, for the colonies did not begin to match England in population, wealth or military power. The division at home aggravated an already serious situation. Then too, the Indians lined up with the British against the Americans.

In 1776, the British fleet arrived in Narragansett Bay and put ashore one thousand men who were quartered in the houses of the citizens. General Prescott, a bully and a tyrant, commanded the forces.

Newport's financial and political dominance over the other Rhode Island towns ceased during the Revolutionary War from 1776 until 1779 when the British occupied the town. Most of Newport sided with the rebel cause and fought bravely. This is when Newport's commercial and cultural activities came to an end. Many families fled Newport, among them a large segment of the Jewish community who helped found the city and contributed greatly to its cultural activities. The population dropped from nine thousand to five thousand.

The Point suffered greatly when the British occupied Newport. Approximately 1100 houses stood in Newport at that time, but during the blockade the British tore down hundreds of buildings to meet the demand for firewood. Many homes bore a large "S" on their chimneys to show that they were British sympathizers, hoping that their homes would be spared. On October 25, 1779, the British evacuated a severely devastated Newport after a savage destruction that left Newport in ruins.

The British destroyed 400 buildings of various classes. They burned the lighthouse at Beavertail, cut down all the ornamental and fruit trees, broke nearly all the wharves, and destroyed all the houses of worship, except for Trinity Church and the Jewish Synagogue. The night that they evacuated the town, under the orders of the British commander, they filled the wells to make them unusable and as much property as possible was destroyed.

The occupation of the French forces under Comte de Rochambeau occurred shortly after. The French arrived on the scene to aid the colonial cause and were welcomed by the long-suffering citizens. Victory was achieved partly because of this aid from overseas. In the French and Indian War, Britain humbled the proud French monarchy. Anxious for revenge, France decided to help the thirteen colonies. In this decision, there was no love for revolution, nor any desire to promote the democratic and republican views of the American colonists. The French court was indeed against such views, but the colonist's rebellion was a way to hurt the hated English.

7. The Touro Synagogue

The Synagogue is not on the Point, but the men who were responsible for erecting this beautiful building and who worshipped there were most definitely an important part of the Point. It was here that many of them built their homes and businesses. Their culture and values were part of the Point. It is to honor them that we tell of their heritage and their contributions.

The first synagogue in America was erected in New York City in 1730. However, it had to yield to the city's growth and it was demolished. As a result, the Newport Synagogue is the oldest existing synagogue in North America.

The design and location of the Newport Synagogue demonstrated that the Jews were comfortable observing their religion in Newport. They were confident that the Gentiles accepted the Jewish presence in Newport's community of religions. It was built in the center of Newport, a short distance from the colonial legislature and courthouse.

They further showed their willingness to conform to colonial aesthetics by choosing Peter Harrison as the architect. He was born in England, but came to Newport in 1740 and became the most notable architect in America in the mid 18th century. It was constructed to serve the spiritual needs of the prosperous Newport Sephardic (Spanish and Portuguese) Jewish community that dated from 1658. Building began in 1757 with the help of Jews throughout the British Empire and was completed in 1763. Isaac Touro was the driving force behind the Newport Synagogue. Until it was dedicated, the Jewish Congregation met in one of their homes on the Sabbath.

According to the custom of Sephardic Jews, the Synagogue was built on a quiet, very inconspicuous street. It was built to stand diagonally on a very small lot. This was done so worshipers in prayer before the Holy Ark face eastward toward Jerusalem.

Inside the gracious building twelve Ionic columns, representing the twelve tribes of Israel, support a gallery. Above these are twelve Corinthian columns that support the domed ceiling. Men and women sit separately, the men on the first floor and the women in the gallery.

Five massive candelabras are suspended from the ceiling. The Eternal Light hangs in front of the Holy Ark. The Ark contains the Scrolls of the Law, or Torah. These scrolls are the most cherished of the Jewish objects for on them are recorded the Five Books of Moses, the basis of the Jewish faith. These were all brought from Europe. Above the Ark, the Ten Commandments are depicted in Hebrew.

At one time the synagogue had an underground passage to the street. This was probably a hiding place and an underground tunnel of escape. It was constructed by people, who in their new world of American freedom, could not forget the sense of persecution and terror that haunted their past.

There was a time when the Spanish Jew lived in a Golden Age. A time when his intellectual and spiritual horizons were unsurpassed, when his economic powers and the grandeur of his culture were unparalleled, but the Golden Age fell.

Three things brought about the downfall: the bigotry of the 12th century, the Christian terror of 1391 and a hundred years later (1491) when the Spanish monarchy and the Spanish church united. The light that was the Spanish Jewry was then forever extinguished.

Some of the Spanish Jews in that year chose Christian baptism rather than exile. However, over one hundred thousand fled to neighboring Portugal preferring the pain of dispersion. Some of these people

Touro Family Gravesite

however were reportedly enslaved a few months after their flight. Five years later (1501) the Portuguese crown compelled all of its Jewish subjects to accept baptism. In 1506, King Mariael decreed their conversion and they found themselves in the midst of a walking nightmare.

The Portuguese contemptuously called them the "New Christians" and were angry because of the economic competition offered by these despised "conversos." A mob in Lisbon took matters into their own hands, attacked them and killed them in great numbers and threw many of them, still half alive, into the furnaces. Two hundred years later the Jewish race in Lisbon still feared persecution.

The first Jews came to Newport in 1658. A few wanderers lived in Newport in sufficient numbers to hold services and buy a cemetery lot. A deed in 1677 granted Jewish burial rights on a street that is now the site of a Jewish cemetery. There were many times and places throughout history when Jews were not allowed to establish cemeteries. The fact that in Newport they could have one persuaded them to remain. For unknown reasons, the congregation dispersed by about 1700. This may have been a consequence of the uncertainties of life in Rhode Island. A new influx began a half-century later when rich and eminent Jews from Portugal and the West Indies arrived and an established Jewish community developed.

In 1754, newcomers formed the Congregation Nephuse Israel (Scattered Ones). Ten years later it was changed to Yeshuat Israel (Salvation of Israel). This change reflected the growth of numbers and wealth, and the sense of finding a home. Within 50 years of their return, the Jewish community found great success in colonial Newport although they were still legally disadvantaged and were politically discriminated against throughout this period.

The Jewish community took root in Newport and had flourished in its tolerant atmosphere. Christian and Jew, although they worshipped separately and in a different language, had the same dreams and aspirations. They met on equal terms in the homes, in business, in society and in the army throughout the 19th century. They were known for their hard work and business acumen. Through their energy and skill these Jews helped to make Newport one of the most cultured and important trading posts of the colonies. With the Quakers, they went on to dominate the town's economy and society. They resided in two areas of Newport, close to their places of business on the Point and the Parade (Washington Square). No Jews lived in the southern section of Newport at that time.

There were many prominent Jewish men in Newport. Isaac Touro, Judah Touro, Abraham Touro and Aaron Lopez were just four among the many who gave so much of themselves both to the Synagogue and to Newport.

However, the Revolution proved most damaging to them and dealt a severe setback to Newport economy. So loyally did most of the Jews support the Revolutionary cause, that when the British did capture the town in 1776, most were forced to flee never again to return to their old homes. By 1791, the Synagogue was virtually closed. The Holy Scrolls were sent to the Congregation Sheath Israel in New York.

On October 5, 1822, Moses Lopez, the last survivor of the Jewish Community left Newport. The second Congregation vanished as completely as the first. Only the empty Synagogue and the neglected cemetery remained. The British, while stripping the entire town for firewood, destroyed about 500 houses, but honored the sanctity of the Synagogue and left it standing.

When they arrived in Newport the French had managed to bring a little glamour to the impoverished colony but when they left there was very little remaining of the once glamorous town. Its scars were deep. Commerce and the Jews had forsaken it. The wharves were deserted, and the lamp in the

Synagogue built in 1762 was extinguished

Closed are the portals of their Synagogue,
No psalms of David now the silence break.
No Rabbi reads the ancient Decalogue
In the grand dialect the Prophets spake.
Gone are the living... but the dead remain,
And not neglected, for a hand unseen
Scattering its bounty, like a summer rain
Still keeps their graves and their remembrance green.

Henry Wadsworth Longfellow.
"The Jews in Rhode Island"

The Synagogue reopened for a short time on October 2, 1850, and religious services were held although not regularly. Then the Synagogue closed again and remained closed except for rare occasions for three decades. During that time, although deserted, it was kept in repair by an agreement with the Trustees of its large fund.

On rare occasions it was opened for weddings or for funerals when the Jews brought back their dead to lay them by the ashes of their forefathers. On one occasion, the Synagogue was opened for a member of the Hart family, a lady of over 80 years of age. She came from Savannah to revisit the Synagogue and sit once more on the seat that she had occupied as a child. She took with her, from the cemetery of her fathers, a handful of earth that was added to her grave in Savannah when she died. In 1830, the Synagogue opened for the funeral services of Moses Lopez who died at the age of 86 in New York. His body was brought back for interment in the cemetery of the Jews. A year later, a steamer brought the body of Rebecca Lopez, the only daughter of Reyna and Isaac Touro, from New York. It was placed in the Synagogue where services were performed and, as she requested, was interred the following day in the Jewish cemetery.

In 1881, restored by the gifts of the brothers Abraham and Judah Touro, sons of Isaac Touro, its old time Huzzan, it again held regular services on High Holy Days. By 1883, there were enough Jewish settlers in Newport to open regularly for Sabbath services. Since 1883, the Synagogue has developed continuously and without interruption. It stands today serene and beautiful in the center of the city. In 1946, it was designated a national treasure. It welcomes visitors from all over the world, both Jew and Gentile.

In 1999, for the first time in its history a woman, Mrs. Aaron (Rita) Slom, was elected President of the Synagogue. Also in that year, Ambassador John L. Loeb, Jr., who claims kinship with the Touros of the past, donated millions of dollars to the Synagogue. His only stipulations were that the new proposed Jewish Visitor's Center in Newport be named after him and that upon his death, he would be buried in the small Jewish Cemetery on the hill at the top of Touro Street, where no one has been buried for over 150 years.

There is opposition to this request by many members of the Jewish community. Although the cemetery was deeded to the Jewish population in 1677, there is no headstone that bears a date prior to 1761, almost a century later. Many of the Jews who were interred in the earlier period may not have had their graves marked. Those graves that did bear markers have, with the passing of time, lost their identification as the stones deteriorated and crumbled into the ground. Without doubt there are many Jews buried here in unmarked graves. It is only right that these graves, marked or unmarked, be left untouched. The site is historical and since no burial has taken place there in 150 years, none should be allowed. As one member of the Jewish community has stated, "Especially not for someone of the modern generation and certainly not for the exchange of silver." Mr. Loeb's connection with the Touro family must be a distant one. All records show that when Judah Touro died, the name of the Touro family died with him. Isaac Touro's three sons and one daughter died childless.

The Synagogue is a plain building on the outside, but everything within is so unique, so enchanting, and so rich in symbolism, words could never truly explain the beauty therein. It holds a place in the hearts of the Jewish people everywhere. It is a testimonial to their faith in God, in America and in their neighbors.

The officers of Touro Synagogue granted permission so that the photographs shown could be taken. It was a memorable moment, standing by the graves of the members of the Jewish religion who contributed so much to our city. Since I had researched for many years the early Jews in Newport, their lives, their hopes, their dreams and their struggles, I stood there in wonderment and awe. I felt a great respect and a sense of belonging to those who finally are at rest in this most unusual and beautiful cemetery.

Chateau Sur Mer

Chateau-sur-Mer was built in 1852 by William S. Wetmore, who made his fortune in the China trade and banking. Lithograph by John Collins, "The City and Scenery of Newport, Rhode Island, 1857."

8. After the Revolution

The disruption and damage of the Revolution put an end to prosperity, to commerce and possibly to ambition, because so many outstanding citizens fled the town. In that conflict, a thriving prosperous society was destroyed after more than a century of uninterrupted growth, when all profitable sea-lanes led to Newport.

Between the years of 1815 and 1828, Newport was in a state of limbo. During these 13 years, not one house was built in the city. One lumberyard supplied all the material needed for repairs and a dozen carpenters found little work. Newport was considered finished. For the next ten years Newporters hoped and waited for the return of the commerce that had been their pride. They waited in vain. Commerce never returned.

Fifty years after the revolution, scarcely a new house had been built in town. From its dreary appearance a visitor would never know that before the war Newport was a community of influence and prosperity. So many houses had been destroyed during the Revolution that the population was reduced to five thousand and many of them had to live together in single dwellings. The city, or what was left of it, was on an island separated from the mainland by water on all sides. All industry was gone. The unemployed stood with folded hands on the street corners, shops had nothing but meager supplies, rags were stuffed in windows to conserve heat, and grass grew unheeded and uncut in the public squares. The spirit of its citizens was as dismal as the town. Efforts to bring back manufacturing failed.

Although the Revolution left Newport desolate, the nation was young. The people relied very heavily on their one asset, the Atlantic Ocean. It was not until the middle of the 19th century that things began to change.

Before 1850, land along the Cliff Walk was pastureland. Ten years before the Civil War, twelve men came to the island for the summer, four from Boston and eight from New York. They built the first of the "summer cottages," the magnificent mansions that are known throughout the world. William Wetmore built the first "cottage" along the Cliffs in 1852.

Sailors filled the harbor once more as Newport began to gain a reputation as a resort community. These were seamen of another type. They were not merchant sailors but rather wealthy men who belonged to the pleasure craft world.

Rich southern planters began to come to the Isle of Peace in their own luxury yachts with their families and servants. Newport's temperatures and picturesque setting attracted them. Newport became increasingly popular as a summer resort. Summer colonists arrived and stayed at the hotels that were built during the 1840s and 1850s. They came from New York, Boston and Philadelphia. Newport attracted the intellectuals, the writers, and the painters who were among the elite of the nation.

While the summers were filled with sports and entertainment of the wealthy, the Newporters themselves struggled to earn enough money to tide them over during the rest of the year. However, in the late 1850s, rumblings of war again filled the air. Many southern families failed to return. It was in Newport that they owned property and socialized, and they were stunned when Newport opposed secession and prepared for war.

Newport in the early 1830s had experienced a time when hotels were built and land speculators bought large tracts of land. This had a great effect on the city's economy and it definitely influenced its future. The Civil War had another profound effect on Newport. It brought the Navy to Newport for the first time. Along with the Vanderbilts, Belmonts, Astors, Morgans and the Goelets.

After the Civil War, the robber barons arrived in what was to become the most fashionable summer resort in the world. Their money was in railroads, coal, furs, mail, packing and shipping, tobacco, silver mines and all the great commodities and service industries of the late 19th century.

One of the natural attractions of Newport is the Cliff Walk that runs three and one half miles along the eastern shoreline. A beautiful area where one can walk along the coastline and watch the ocean and its ever changing tides.

It was along this coastline that the wealthy built their mansions. In 1874, there were 500 cottages and villas in the city. Thus began the "Golden Era." It was a time of unbridled materialism. Money flowed like wine, there was no income tax, servants were plentiful, and they worked long hours and received little pay. Most lived-in. Fortunes were made, flaunted and enjoyed to the point of excess. It was a modern day Babylon. Socially ambitious women attempting to outdo each other in spending and entertainment made Newport's opulence and extravagance world famous. Snobbery was at its height. Unrestrained materialism was rampant.

However, these showplaces did not overwhelm the city itself. They were built in a suburb by the Atlantic Ocean, cloistered and isolated, beyond the boundaries of the town, leaving the colonial city nestled on Narragansett Bay.

Newport could count among her blessings a wonderful climate and a splendid harbor. The coming of the railroad and coastal steamers made real estate between Boston and New York most desirable. Newport was at its prime when the railroad was extended to the city in 1863. Its fame crossed the ocean and distinguished foreigners came to see for themselves what was known as the chosen resort of the rich and philosophic.

Newport was able to boast of the culture of its people. Redwood Library was second only to Harvard. The schools were the finest. The year 1900 found the Golden Age of Newport at its peak. Unfortunately nothing lasts forever.

As the prosperity of the colonial merchants collapsed after the Revolution that destroyed the town, so too, the wealthy were humbled by the enforcement of an income tax in 1913 and World War I. Fortunes were lost in the Wall Street crash of 1929. The newly formed unions that protected the working class and the imposition of estate tax and rising property taxes splintered the large fortunes. No longer was their money tax free. No longer could they employ their servants for a pittance.

The Great Depression of the 1930s had a gradual impact on Newport. It brought an end to the era. Income tax and the pressure of rising costs caused the loss of the summer colony. Since the great homes required large staffs of indoor and outdoor servants, they could rarely be used all year long and the unions brought to an end the supply of inexpensive help. Newport's mansions were to become "White elephants" and the many Newporters who serviced these show places were now unemployed. Mansions were sold for a pittance or given to a charitable organization. The Newport Torpedo Station closed when World War II ended. This caused the loss of thousands of jobs.

All these events caused neglect to many of the homes in Newport as well as those on the Point. Colonial Newport fell into disrepair. For a long time Newport slept and there was little to bring back the former prosperity. However, the personal poverty that resulted may have protected the city from the more devastating forms of progress and we doubtless owe the existence of our colonial homes to that very personal poverty.

There was no industrialization and therefore no pressure to tear down and rebuild. During the war there was an intense demand for housing for the workforce, and so many of the older houses in need of repairs were spared.

So in the late 1930s, we find Newport a city with little activity, little income, and a great many houses covering a wide period of time from the late 17th century to the 20th. These finest examples of American architecture were in desperate need of repair. Once again Newport rallied.

Naval Training Station

9. The United States Navy

Naval forces have been associated with Newport history for more than 300 years. From colonial times, when the Royal Navy first sailed into Narragansett Bay, through the Civil War that brought the U.S. Navy to Newport for the first time. At that time, the Naval Academy was moved from Annapolis to Newport as a precautionary measure. Although the Academy remained for only four years, the Navy fleet was here to stay. Its presence has always been a great factor in the prosperity of the area from World War II, when the military changed the face of Newport, until today's modern fully equipped, education oriented Naval Base.

With the Civil War over, the old fort on Goat Island was equipped with a laboratory and factory for the manufacture and testing of torpedoes and other new weapons. The year was 1869 and the Naval Torpedo Station was born.

In 1883, Commodore Steven Luce established the Naval Training Station on Coaster's Harbor Island. Before the Training Station was established, Navy recruits received no formal education. They learned their trade on ships at sea. The following year Luce established the Naval War College in a building that once housed the deaf and dumb asylum called "The Poor House." This is now "Founders Hall" and the site of the War College Museum.

Newport's naval bases were at full peak during 1938 as the nation again prepared for the eventuality of war that became a reality in 1941.

During World War II, housing for many military personnel and their families was critical. It was then that Newport landlords, both in a patriotic and mercenary manner, turned many of the single-family homes into apartments.

The influx of military families offered landlords with financial problems the opportunity to recover some of the losses they suffered during the Depression. Any available space was utilized but many of the tenants who stayed for short military duty did not really appreciate the history or the workmanship of the homes. These souvenirs of Newport's greater days were beginning to go to wrack and ruin. Yet these homes, during the War years, sheltered many servicemen and their families from around the world.

Great friendships began and endured. Servicemen from far off cities and countries met, fell in love with, and married local girls. Local boys went afar, met girls from many foreign countries, fell in love and brought them home as brides. Many again made Newport their permanent home. Other Navy men who had served here found the city irresistible and, having finished their tours of duty, returned and retired here. From Basic Seaman to Admiral, Newport has become "home" to these veterans.

Servicemen by the thousands trained at the Naval Training Station and Coddington Point. They walked through the Point to arrive at the center of Newport where movie theaters and bars were the chief entertainment. It was a lively time. The USO helped the homesick and lonely so far from home.

In 1945 with the war's end, Newport faced large unemployment. The Naval Base downscaled. The Torpedo Station went onto a skeleton force and eventually closed completely. Many people were out of work. Property became even more neglected. Exteriors soon became an eyesore. Businesses closed and the once thriving center of the city became deserted. Only the Newport Daily News remained in the downtown area. It was like a ghost town.

Once again Newport was to face a severe loss. It was a political decision when, in 1971, a large segment of the Navy left Newport. Although the education center, the world famous War College and many of the ships remained, the loss of the larger part of the fleet was a devastating blow to Newport.

The Point became "quiet" and Newport missed the Navy and their activities. The bugle notes still waken the Point residents in the morning when the wind is right. Taps still sound at eventide, but the everyday Navy is gone. The War College renowned throughout the world, the Surface Warfare School, the Justice School, and the Chaplain's School have remained. These are officers or potential officers, trained in the different schooling systems. They have their own cars or bicycles. They rarely walk through the Point to reach the Training Station. They now drive on the highways that were constructed during and after the war. This new breed jogs through the Point in groups of three or four. No longer do the Squadrons march from the Station, through the Point, to give a public demonstration at Washington Square.

In March 1993, it was announced that Newport would lose the last of its naval ships. They have been here since our very beginning, and it will be a different place without them. The world is supposed to be at peace and its demands today are different. We require only a smaller military structure and that is the Educational Navy. They are all fine schools. Newport will always be a Navy town, but the sailors and the destroyers are gone forever. Sadly, in the summer of 1994 the last of the ships left Newport.

10. Restoration of Newport

During the war years some of the landlords, knowing they had a large list of prospective tenants, hiked rents and neglected their property. Many of the once proud homes on "The Point" started to decline. Their property became even more neglected when the war ended. With rent control now in effect, the exteriors soon became an eyesore.

The Preservation Society was created in 1945 by Mrs. George Henry Warren to protect the Hunter House. Private citizens organized to rescue the finer homes and mansions that they then restored and opened for public viewing. Today, if you stroll down Bellevue Avenue the mansions are still there, the gardens are just as beautiful, the gaslights glow in the evening. These mansions now belong to the public who, for a fee, may wander through the rooms. You may close your eyes, and imagine that you live in this glorious home, or visualize what it was like before when the Vanderbilts and the Astors lived in it. They probably watched the sun rise over the ocean; thought that their lives would go on forever, that the ball would never end. The ball finally ended and Newport suffered as the mansions fell into disrepair. The Preservation Society was the first organization to begin the restoration of this lovely town.

In the early 1960s an English lady, Nadine Pepys, became interested in the neglected smaller colonial homes. She, with others, formed "CLAPBOARD," an association dedicated to restore many of the Point homes to their original beauty. Houses that were sold to CLAPBOARD for $3,000 to $10,000 now command prices up to $400,000. CLAPBOARD did not restore the houses. They simply purchased them and held the houses until they could locate prospective buyers who could and would have the finances and the ability to renovate these homes and this they did.

The Old Port Association, a non-profit organization, followed in 1963 with Tom Benson as collaborator. This organization acquired houses and functioned as a clearinghouse for those who wished to purchase and restore a home for their own residence. It was formed with the object of keeping intact, as far as was possible, the charm of the Point section.

Doris Duke provided unlimited funds, knowledge and craftsmen for the effort founded the Newport Restoration Foundation in 1965. This foundation purchases the homes, and retains ownership. It then leases them in order to retain control of the historical accuracy of the restoration and preservation. These organizations changed the face of Newport for the better.

Though the Point, for the most part remained unchanged, in the 1960s the State and Federal Government combined to finance the Newport-Jamestown Bridge. Despite efforts to prevent this, the bridge was built. It cut a swath through the oldest part of Newport, destroying some of the beautiful homes in the Washington Street, Bayside Avenue, Cypress and Third Street area. This left the beautiful bay with a bridge marring the once wide-open view. The bridge, a spectacular man-made achievement was dedicated in June 1969. Its main span is 1600 feet making it the longest suspension bridge in New England. Its total length is 2.13 miles. Its opening brought the demise of the Jamestown ferry. It also opened Newport to more commercialization. To most Point Hummers, this was a tragedy.

Newport Bridge

Newport mourned the death of Doris Duke in 1994. She contributed so much time, effort and money to the restoration of these lovely houses. Without her gracious assistance we would probably never have attained so much. Upon her death, all of the houses that she assisted in restoring bore yellow ribbons to honor her. However, not all the homes have been restored. There is still a great deal to do. The Point is a family and all its members work to help each other for the benefit of all.

Corner of Bridge St. and Washington St. Restored by the Newport Restoration Foundation

11. The Liberty Tree

In a sacred garden in Sri Lanka, there stands a truly enormous tree over 2,000 years old. It is twice as old as the Conqueror's Oak in Windsor Forest, England and a hundred years older than the olive trees in the Garden of Gethsemane. It is probably the most venerable of all the trees in the world.

The Greeks believed that trees have perception, passions and reason. Primitive people were said to worship them as gods. Our ancestors lived in clearings in the virgin forest where the trunks of these beautiful trees furnished them with wood for their dwellings and under whose sheltering shade they found rest and relief. It is natural that in their minds the trees had imaginary powers. So is it not surprising that a mighty old tree is looked upon with awe and is an object of respect and reverence?

As we stand at the triangular park at the corner of Thames and Farewell Street, known as William Ellery Park or "Liberty Park," we can view the spot where the citizens planted the first Liberty tree on the street outside the park. William Ellery was one of the signers of the Declaration of Independence whose home stood across the street.

The Sons of Liberty planted the original tree, a buttonwood, in 1766 to symbolize opposition to the Stamp Act and the resistance of Newport to British aggression. The British cut it down when they arrived in 1776.

Several years later when the British left Newport, a second tree was planted and rededicated in 1783. A copper plate with the names of the thirteen men who joined in its restoration was affixed to this second tree in 1823. Over the years the copper became covered by the bark of the tree. On anniversaries the tree was illuminated with 365 glass lanterns. Each lantern held three candles. A total of 1,095 candles were illuminated on the tree at one time.

This tree was still standing in 1857 and did so until the 1860s. It became very decayed and was believed to have been struck by lightning. The only solution was to cut it down. The copper plate was removed and is now in the possession of the Newport Historical Society.

A third tree, a new oak, was planted in 1876 but this failed to thrive. In 1897 the fourth tree, a healthy young fern beech, was planted with these words:

"The Liberty Tree. May it bring forth its branches until it shall meet the sun in its home and may the light of the departing day linger among its branches. May the young child be taught to venerate the principle and the men who planted the first tree here. Let no rude hand molest it; may it resist the storms of winter and under the mild influence of Spring bring forth the new buds of promise; may this spot always be held sacred for the same purpose and when this tree shall decay may another be put in its place."

The fourth tree was moved from the street to its present site within the park in 1918.

The Liberty Tree

The tree was remembered in the following poem:

"They are all gone.. all gone" it seems to say.
"They are in their graves and I should not stay.
The stout old hands that have planted me here
Have been mouldering now for many a year.
Their children and their children's children I have seen

44

Laid down in the shade of my branches green.
That stalwart race is gone from the land
And why should I any longer stand?
To royal equals, too, of the wood
Who in other days around me stood,
The motherly elm and the fatherly oak
Have bowed to decay or the woodsman's stroke.
The poplar, the beech and the dark green ash
Have startled the fields with their farewell crash.
They have left me here in my solitude
O'er the memories of the best to brood,
And under my present misery
A proud old naked and useless tree
Oh men who have hearts of flesh (I pray)
That the words of a poor old tree can feel,
Come to my help with the merciful steel
Come with your axes and lay me low.
They are gone and it is time that I too should go.
Build in the chimney my funeral pyre
And let me mount on wings of fire
To crown with deathless green the shore
Where the fathers are gathered forevermore."

Songs of Field and Flood
Rev. C. T. Brooks

The medallion pictured below, was issued on May of 1976 commemorating the 200th anniversary of Rhode Island Independence. On one side the Aquidneck Island is shown and on the other side appears the Liberty Tree with the words "Undaunted by tyrants, we'll die or be free."

Liberty Park has given pleasure to thousands of children who, over the years, played on, under and around the tree. A small fountain stood in the center of the park. Children were warned not to climb the tree not only for the fear of injury but also because they might harm the branches and cause damage to the tree. But climb it they did. Today the tree flourishes. However, the park is entirely fenced in, the fountain and the benches removed, and seldom does anyone enter. There it stands, the lovely tree, spreading its branches, so full, so tall, but there are no children, no laughter, and no pets to enjoy its cool shade.

What happened to the men and women who planted the tree? Those who fought for our freedom and those who came later; those who sat on the benches, read the papers purchased from the little store that later stood on what had been William Ellery's land. What happened to the large families, immigrants mostly, who lived around the park, the Irish, English, Portuguese, French, German, African, Jewish? Some of these people are still here in Newport, others are thousands of miles away, and many have died. For those who would again view this small park and lovely tree, we know it would bring memories of those happy times, of carefree days, and of loving families. It will also bring feelings of sadness, memories of those whom we have loved and lost.

12. Houses

You never really own a house. It is yours only for a time. There were others who came before you and others who will come after you. When the floorboard creaks or the wind whistles in the chimney, old houses whisper of past lives. They whisper of the children who ran up and down the stairs, of the women and servants who cooked in the open hearths that may still be there boarded up, and of the forgotten men who built these homes. They whisper of all those who lived within, and who lived and loved and dreamed. Who were these people of the past?

THE HOUSE

WHO LIVED HERE BEFORE I CAME,
WHO LIVED IN THIS ROOM,
HOW DID IT LOOK, WAS IT THE SAME?

WAS THERE A GIRL OR TWO, A LITTLE BOY,
A HOUSE FILLED WITH TOYS,
WITH JOYS, WITH DREAMS?

OR WAS I T JUST A LONELY PLACE,
WITH EMPTY BEDS AND SILENT ROOMS
WAS IT ALWAYS FILLED WITH GLOOM?

AND DID THE HOUSE LONG TO BE LOVED,
WAS THERE A GIRL WHO DANCED AND SANG,
A DINNER BELL THAT CHIMED OR RANG?

AND DID ANYONE EVER STAND RIGHT HERE,
AS I DO NOW,
DO I KNOW THE NAME, HAVE I SEEN THE FACE....
WAS THIS ALWAYS THE SAME SWEET PLACE?

WAS SOMEONE GLAD, WAS SOMEONE SAD,
WAS THERE A DOG, A CAT, A HORSE, A MOUSE,
WHO HAS BEEN HERE, WHO KNOWS THIS HOUSE?

DO THEY KNOW ME, DO I KNOW THEM.
AND DID THEY SING A REQUIEM?
I FEEL THEM HERE, I KNOW THEIR FEARS,
I LOVED THEM TOO.

THE HOUSE WAS NEW, WAS THEIRS, WAS DIFFERENT THEN
AND YET IT IS THE SAME AGAIN,
AND WAS, AND WILL, AND MUST ALWAYS BE,
AND NOW THE HOUSE BELONGS TO ME.

Author Unknown

The Plymouth House - Butterfly Tavern, 53 Farewell Street

This house was on the eastern side of Liberty Park. Mr. and Mrs. Robert Queriot once owned it during the 1930s. The delightful three-story building no longer stands. The spot holds many memories for all who ever lived in the area.

The Plymouth House was a boarding house for the actors and actresses who performed at the local theaters. It was home to others but somehow the colorful and exciting lives of the performers took precedence and it will always be remembered for the unusual and diverse experiences these people added to our lives.

There were midgets, clowns, talented dancers, actors, acrobats, singers and comedians who, during off hours, strolled throughout the neighborhood. They sat in Liberty Park across the street where the neighborhood children played, roller skated and generally caused mischief.

There were fortunetellers who would teasingly entice the children to run home "to wash their hands" so that their fortunes could be told. Invariably, when the child returned the fortuneteller would be gone.

The neighborhood around this house was a most congenial one. The families of many origins intermingled, as did the children. It was a great educational experience. There were neighborhood fights among the children, but they learned the principles of give and take. The neighborhood "cop" would hold the children's hands as they learned to skate around the sharp curve of the Park. Neighbors experienced all sorts of excellent cuisine. Parents shared the different ethnic dishes, breads, cookies, etc., with the neighborhood children as well as with their own. It was truly the "League of Nations" and families and children stayed friends throughout the decades.

The Plymouth House was torn down in the 1960s and a colonial saltbox was moved from the southern end of Newport, via the harbor, to the Poplar Street pier. It was then, slowly and carefully, trucked to the empty lot. The saltbox was then known as "The Pilot House." However, in the early 1700s, it was a tavern on Washington Street near Battery Park known as the Butterfly Tavern and later the Battery Tavern. It was then moved to Long Wharf. Again in 1851, it was moved across the bay to Houston Avenue. It served many purposes but fell into a state of disrepair. It was rescued by Pilot Captain Bruce Fisher and brought back to the Point, where it now sits on the site of the once well-known Plymouth House.

It is now the residence of Mercedes Deines.

The Cozzens House, 57-59 Farewell Street

This beautiful duplex Colonial stands on the Northeast corner of Farewell and Warner Street. The earliest record shows that the land was owned by Timothy Balch who sold it to brothers William and

Joseph Cozzens who, sometime in the 1770s, built the house. The two and a half story house has two interior chimneys. Each side is a mirror image of the other. It was one of the first double houses ever built in America. There are many fascinating stories about this house and its occupants for it has had many owners and renters over the years.

In 1787, Paul Cartwright purchased it. Many families followed: Langley, Northam and Stevens. It was in the Stevens family for many years after the Revolution so that it is also known as the William Stevens House.

In the 1800s it was known as the house with the "Faces on the Fence Posts." It was rumored that a family was murdered in the north side of the building (the side that borders the cemetery) and that their faces periodically appeared on the finials of the fence posts. In the 1800s such stories were accepted. Superstition was rampant.

In the 1900s, a young Irish colleen was living in the house and heard the stories. She awoke the household one night with her screams of " a woman's face on her pillow." This was the time when women took discarded flour sacks, washed and bleached them and then used them as pillowcases. The face on the pillow proved to be the face of the lady symbolized on the Gold Medal flour sacks. Another legend tells of the runaway slave who fearing that he was to be reclaimed hung himself in the attic.

During the 1930s, Irish immigrant John Danahy owned the home with his wife and three daughters and lived in it for many years. It had been converted into a number of tenements and the Danahys lived in one. The property was maintained during his lifetime but after Mr. Danahy's death his daughters sold the house and it deteriorated with the passing years. It became quite run down and in the early 1950s was an eyesore and occupied mainly by welfare families. In 1952, the city records deemed it "in bad condition."

Olcott Smith, a friend of one of the descendents of the Cozzen's family, purchased the home in the early 1960s and completely restored it.

In 1967, Commander and Mrs. Richard Alsager purchased it and made further renovations. Today this remarkable and stately house stands in its former splendor, a truly beautiful home. One side is occupied by its owners, Mr. and Mrs. Douglas Riggs (Mrs. Riggs is the former Mary Alsager.)

The story of the faces on the fence posts has never been forgotten and it is revived whenever Halloween draws near or a "ghost" story is told.

The Rebecca Inn, 15 Thames Street

This charming Victorian was once owned by one of the first freed slaves. In later years it passed into the hands of Dr. and Mrs. Saunders. Dr. Saunders had his office in the rear of the house.

The land extended from Thames to Cross Street and was one of the larger parcels in the area. It was an enormous house known as the Thames Street Mansion. It consisted of four living rooms and a huge kitchen with a stone fireplace that reached from floor to ceiling. There were seven bedrooms and a full attic and when the Saunders sisters lived there it was full of toys. When Dr. Saunders died, his two sons and his one married daughter relinquished their rights in the estate in favor of their two unmarried sisters, who were Newport schoolteachers.

These two sisters resided in the home for many, many years to the delight of the neighborhood children. On rainy days if they were good, they were allowed to play on the third floor with all the toys.

The house had a large porch where neighbors waited, especially on rainy and windy days, for the trolley that passed by the front door. This porch was removed during the war years when, after the Misses Saunders passed away, the house was purchased by Dorothy and George Savard. They turned it into a rooming house with a beauty parlor on the first floor.

William and Eileen Nimmo purchased the building in 1967, as it had always been a favorite of theirs. Eileen played there as a child. They renamed it "The Rebecca Inn" after their niece, Rebecca Hayes Andrews.

52

However, times were rapidly changing in Newport in the 60s as in other parts of the country. They feared further deterioration of the neighborhood, which they loved and wished to preserve. With that thought in mind they sold this gracious home to Operation Clapboard when the first redevelopment to preserve these lovely historical homes began.

It stands today, as originally intended, a beautiful one family home, the residence of Mr. and Mrs. Gary Fay. It boasts a lovely cupola on top and perhaps one day it will again have a porch facing Thames Street.

The Braman House, 18 Thames Street

This most unique home was the birthplace of the author. Built about 1715, the first known deed of record was in 1774 when the Widow Johnson sold the property to David Braman, a caulker, who had a number of houses. The house was situated with the front door on the south side, perhaps because the lot was too narrow to accommodate it otherwise. Post-medieval English style, it was made of heavy construction and the second floor bedroom has gunstock posts.

The original house was probably built as two rooms over two rooms. During the later 1800s, walls were partitioned to provide separate bedrooms that were very small. An addition was added to the back to allow for indoor bathrooms and it became a two-family home and was rented as such for many years while still the property of the Braman estate.

This pre-revolutionary house had a trap door that lifted from a closet off the kitchen to allow for hidden access to the cellar. The original door with its wide planks has been removed and a newer trap door, in a more accessible spot in the kitchen itself, has replaced it. The kitchen was spacious while bedrooms were small and closets were non-existent. The cellar was not tall enough to stand upright in and had an uneven dirt floor.

The property remained in the Braman family until 1953. It was then transferred to Packer Braman who sold it, the following year, to George and Alice Callahan. Mrs. Callahan had been a secretary in Mr. Braman's office for many years.

Braman House Living Room

In 1969, the Newport Restoration Foundation purchased it. It is reported to have been the favorite of Doris Duke, who personally oversaw the details of its restoration. Fully restored in 1971, it is truly one of the most attractive of the colonial homes.

Today, owned by the Newport Restoration Foundation, it is the residence of Mrs. Joanne Salvo, who is the owner of the Simeon Potter Home.

John Stevens Shop, 29 Thames Street

This two-story gambrel roof building is the oldest shop in the country still engaged in the same work at the same location. The shop was founded in 1705. The first John Stevens, born in England in 1646, came from the village of Oxfordshire to Boston in the year 1700.

John Stevens was 53 years of age when he married his young wife, Mercy, and he fathered ten children before he died at the age of 89. In 1709, four years after coming to Newport, he built his home at 30 Thames Street, opposite the shop, and practiced his trade as a stonemason. Soon he began to supply gravestones.

His son, John II, was born in Boston in 1702, the eldest child of the ten. Young John considered himself a bricklayer and he worked on many of Newport's treasured buildings such as Touro synagogue, Redwood Library, the old Congregational Church and the Brick Market. Half of the central chimneys of the Newport houses are his work. He was associated with his father and he was very talented at carving gravestones. Like his father, he married late for an 18th century man at the age of 43.

John III was born in 1754, the youngest child of John II. He seemed to have been especially talented. Some of his most original and best work was done in his early teens, possibly as early as 13. Having neither the desire nor the physique for the more strenuous trades of his forebears, he confined himself strictly to carving. A passionate patriot he could also be Puritanical. He was happy and yet at times very melancholy, gay but yet serious. His "portrait" stones with their graceful borders and fine lettering show an amazing proficiency and a sensitive thoughtfulness.

On December 25, 1783, John III married Mary Shepard. He was 29. By then the Revolution was over. Being exceptionally patriotic, he was one of the young men who carried the second Liberty tree by night from Middletown and planted it at the head of Thames Street, just a few houses from where he lived. On his wedding day, which most likely took place at the Congregational Meeting House, the bride and groom returned to the old homestead on upper Thames Street to candlelight and the fiddler's music. A Thames Street that was then lined with the gracious houses of its merchants, mariners, craftsmen and artisans.

It is known that the Stevens did own slaves and there is evidence that African slave Pompe Stevens, also known as "Zingo" Stevens, worked at the shop and did carve at least two headstones. One was for his brother Cuffe Gibbs, who is believed to be the slave of George Gibbs. Zingo may have produced more stones and, if so, they are unsigned and are probably located in the Common burial ground.

The Revolution left Newport poorer and John II died leaving young John with a widowed mother and family of his own to support. Nontheless, he was a master of lettering. The struggle to make ends meet may have taken its toll. After the death of John III, a succession of Stevenses carried on the work of the shop until 1912 when the last one, Edwin, died.

By that time, the business was bought by John Howard Benson who today is recognized as the finest designer of carved stone lettering in America. In 1927, the business was almost finished. Benson, a noted calligrapher, revived the art of stone cutting by re-establishing the valuable art of Newport's heritage. A very tall, slender man, John Howard Benson was above all a "gentle" man. While running the shop, he also taught at the Rhode Island School of Design.

After his death in 1956, Mrs Benson took over the reins until their son, another John (John Fisher Benson) could follow in his father's footsteps. This he did in a most admirable fashion. When President John F. Kennedy was assassinated the John Stevens Shop, out of all the stonecutters in America, was chosen to carve the inscription on the Kennedy memorial to be placed in Arlington Cemetery. John "Fud" Benson and his son, Nicholas, were the stone carvers for the black granite monument, which was dedicated at a memorial in Montgomery, Alabama to the memory of those who died in the Civil Rights Movement. The shop is known for many other prestigious inscriptions throughout America.

Today it is in the caring hand of Nicholas Benson, the third generation of Bensons.

Callendar School, Willow Street

This large stone school was built during the Presidency of Abraham Lincoln.

Callendar School and Potter School were built exclusively for the education of the Point children. The Callendar School was enlarged in 1900 but in 1974 it was discontinued as a school. After years of being vacant and slowly deteriorating, it was sold in 1980.

The new owners, William and Greta Boggs engaged thirty-three year old Professor Ronalli of the Yale School of Architecture as a designer of six choice condominiums of Italian design, each differentiated by a unique name. These condominiums have now replaced the classrooms. Bedrooms, bathrooms and inglenooks have not disrupted the original structure. Instead of living rooms, galleries overlooked by balconies, are the focal points of each unit.

Much to the credit of the owners, the impressive exterior was not altered, rather it was repaired and the trim painted. The interior was not gutted. Its original design was maintained. Externally it appears as it always was and is now in excellent condition. The former schoolyard is a parking area for the owners. Once bristling with activity, now one rarely observes any movement around it.

The Point no longer has a school for neighborhood children. Busing is now the mode of transportation. This is one instance on the Point where the modern world has displaced the past.

The Old Schoolhouse, 71 Third Street

Walking along Third Street, as you near Pine Street, look closely and you will see a remarkable piece of history. Sitting unnoticed, on a tiny parcel of land, is a small clapboard house. It once had a belfry but that is no longer there.

This little house, built prior to 1796, once stood at the corner of Barney Street and Mt. Vernon Street.

It was a school for colored children, which was discontinued, in the early 1800s. In 1805 Eleazor Trevett, a schoolmaster, moved his school from Clarke Street to the Barney Street location. Evidently he purchased the building at this time. The Trevett School was discontinued sometime in the 1820s.

In 1828 a Catholic priest, Father Woodley, rented the former Barney Street schoolhouse for the first Roman Catholic Church in Rhode Island. There were quite a few Irish Catholics in Newport at that time. In 1830, a more pretentious edifice was built on Sherman Street and dedicated in 1837. St. Mary's and St. Joseph's churches were to follow years later.

Therefore, this little house can claim the distinction of being the "Cradle of the Catholic Church in Rhode Island." Adjacent to the church on Sherman Street was, and is still today, an Irish Catholic Cemetery, which contains some gravestones that are 200 years old.

In 1850, when Mr. Trevett sold the land on Barney Street, he purchased land on the Cherry Street side of the present Stella Maris. The little house with the belfry was then moved to Cherry Street. In 1852, the Quakers began to sell parcels of the land they owned from Walnut Street to the Hunter property and from the east side of Third Street to Long Lane (Farewell Street). There was no railway at this time and the land was entirely barren of houses.

In 1852, Clarke Weaver purchased two acres from the Quakers. This included all the land from the east side of Third Street to the Braman Cemetery, from Cherry Street, north to La Salle Place. In July, 1853 this property passed to his son Thomas. Between 1853 and 1863 the little house was once more moved. This time it was moved to 71 Third Street and it became the home of Thomas Weaver and his family. It remained in the Weaver family until 1912 when it was sold at auction to Mary Nelson. As the years passed the house had many owners and renters.

Now the property of Mr. Frank Sheekey, it sits close to the sidewalk. People pass and hardly notice this inspiring little house that served so many, so well.

Dyre's Gate, Third Street

This is an area near the northern end of Third Street across from Sycamore Street. It once comprised six houses, four duplexes and two cottages, laid out in a horseshoe style. It was so named for Mary and William Dyre. Mary, a Quaker martyr, came to Newport from Providence. Raised in England, she married William Dyer, her cousin, in London, England on October 27, 1633. In 1635 she, with her husband and infant son, immigrated to Boston. She allied herself with Anne Hutchinson in the belief that trust in God is more important than obedience to laws.

Quakers were considered dangerous in England in the 17th century where they were flogged, deported and even hanged. When the Quakers fled England to come to the colonies, they hoped for a more tolerant religious atmosphere. In Massachusetts, the Puritans were even less tolerant. When Anne Hutchinson was expelled from Boston and came to Portsmouth, Rhode Island, Mary and William followed. In 1638, the Dyres moved to Newport where they became one of the towns leading families.

When a settlement in Newport was decided, William Dyre was one of the four chosen to apportion the land and lay out the town. In the year 1640, he was granted 87 acres of land that ran from the now Connell Highway on the East, on a diagonal line to the North of the Blue Rocks then out to Coddington's Corner, now known as Coddington Point. It was named "Dyre's Point." They built their home on what is now the grounds of the Naval Hospital. They were the first family to settle on the Point.

A gate that allowed access to the home was in the area of the present Dyre's Gate and this is why this complex was so named. Farewell Street and Long Lane (now Connell Highway) were highways in those days and this road ended at the byway to Dyre's farm. Third Street was known as the road to "Dyre's Farm." The Dyre family burial ground was on this land.

Mary returned to England in 1650, where William later joined her on colony business. Although he returned, Mary stayed for several years in which time she became a Quaker and a minister of the Society. On their way back to Rhode Island, she passed through Boston where she was arrested and imprisoned. She was not released until William promised that she would speak to no one until she reached the Rhode Island border. After her release, she persisted in returning to Boston to visit imprisoned Quakers and two years later in 1659 she was again arrested. She was banished again and warned that she would be hanged if she ever returned. Within a month she was back, arrested and sentenced to be hanged.

On the day of her execution, the crowd was so great that the bridge between Boston and the North End broke under the weight of the crowd. Mary was led to the gallows that was a giant elm on Boston Common. Her arms were bound and her skirts tied around her ankles. She was made to watch while her companions were executed. She ascended the ladder and a handkerchief was placed over her face.

At the last minute she was reprieved on the condition that she would never again return to Massachusetts. She returned to Rhode Island but, being Mary, she again returned to Boston a few months later demanding fair treatment for her fellow Quakers. Arrested again she was tried and sentenced to be hanged. She was offered her freedom if she would leave and not return. She answered: "Nay, I cannot; for in obedience to the will of the Lord I came and in His work I abide faithful to the end."

Mary Dyre was hanged June 1, 1660, and buried in an unmarked grave on the Boston Common. Following her death the King of England banned all further executions of Quakers in Boston.

William and Mary had seven children. After her death William returned to Newport. He married a second time (Catherine) and had a daughter Elizabeth. Betty Dyre ran the farm that eventually was purchased by the late Charles Hunter who opened it and made it into streets. One of his daughters, Mrs. Thomas Dunn, built one of the finest houses in Newport on a portion of this property.

The Hanging of Mary Dyre
Courtesy of the Newport Historical Society

This was the site of the first theatre production in Rhode Island. Despite the opposition of the Newport clergy, who believed that a theatre was 'sinful' the royalists permitted a playhouse to be built at Dyre's Gate.

In 1853, Robert Maitland built his mansion within 70 feet of the foundation of the old Dyre house where the remains of the foundation and parts of the old stone wall were still visible. On October 25, 1889 while laying out a cross street by the Maitland estate, it became necessary to remove the Dyre family cemetery from what is now the entrance to the Naval Hospital.

When the Newport bridge was constructed three of these houses were razed, taken by eminent domain. The picturesque quality of the complex was utterly destroyed with the removal of the houses. The complex was sliced in half and a large off-ramp was constructed to divert the traffic from the bridge to Newport proper. The construction of the bridge definitely destroyed this section of the Point and changed the entire face and lifestyle of Newport.

Today Dyre's Gate is the only reminder that William and Mary Dyre lived here on the Point over 300 years ago.

Snug Harbor, 1 Sycamore Street

This adorable gambrel roofed house was once a "pest house" used to care for sick people. It was moved from the corner of Van Zandt Avenue and Farewell Street to its present site sometime between 1893 and 1907. At that time the Sherman family owned it. It later became the property the Simpson family who lived on the Point and rented the little cottage to Mr. and Mrs. John Barton. They resided in it for many years with their son John, Jr.

Mr. Barton, a retired Navy man, named it "Snug Harbor" as he felt it was his harbor after many years at sea. On the front door a carefully designed crab served as a doorknocker. Mr. Barton carved it from an old inkwell and it is now in the possession of a granddaughter.

Their three granddaughters, although they did not actually live in the home, made its rooms merry with their presence. Everyone loved Mrs. Barton who took such lovely care of the house and who always made sure that her sidewalks were swept and clean. We can see her still standing in her doorway conversing with all who passed. She was always cheerful and friendly. She worked at the Newport Hospital for many years and every baby girl left the hospital with a ribbon on her head as a token of Mrs. Barton's caring. Mr. Barton planted lovely flowers that were always in abundance around the house. It is said that on the day of his funeral the flowers were never more beautiful.

The State took a portion of this land on Third Street to widen the existing street. It also took property behind the house in order to build a portion of the Newport exit ramp of the bridge. The area within the Sycamore, Cypress, Bayside, Second and Washington streets took the brunt of the change with the construction of the bridge. A once beautiful area was destroyed in the name of progress.

Mr. and Mrs. Walter T. Calcutt now own this home.

The Chester Minkler House, 3 Sycamore Street

This is not a pre-Revolutionary house but this small house was once home to a brilliant man and his wife for more than fifty years. His name was Chester Minkler. He was born in Newport on July 1, 1882, one of the three sons of Edward Wanton Minkler and Charlotte Taylor Minkler. His paternal Dutch ancestors came from the Hudson River area of New York and his maternal ancestors were

Rhode Islanders for many generations. William Townsend, Thomas Goddard (the famous cabinet makers), and William Ellery (a signer of the Declaration of Independence) were ancestors or relatives.

Neighbors knew him as a reticent, modest and kind man who kept to himself. His wife, a stately woman, usually wore an apron over her dress and had a friendly smile for all. To this quiet, tall, thin man with dark hair and gray eyes, our country and its citizens owe much. His brilliance contributed to our safety and well-being.

Chester's father was a clerk and a bookkeeper before he began employment at the Naval Torpedo Station in Newport in 1887. When his father died in 1898, Mrs. Minkler moved with her sons to the Point section of the city, settling first on Cherry Street and then on Third Street.

Educated in the Newport Public Schools, Chester was not able to finish high school. At the age of 16 he left school and secured a job at the Naval Torpedo Station to help with the family finances. Always interested in explosives he had experimented with guncotton and nitroglycerin much to the dismay of his parents. He was a daring young man. When he obtained a job at the Torpedo Station his natural abilities came into play. Many of the experiments he conducted were very dangerous but he seemed to have no fear. He would pull the string from an explosive or would climb out on the wing of an airplane and dislodge a bomb.

A very private person, he was self-taught in mechanical engineering, drafting, naval warfare and history. He was respected by coworkers and friends and devoted his life to his work.

In 1907, he married Gertrude Braman. In 1915, they built the little home at 3 Sycamore Street on land that Gertrude's father gave them. Over the garage, they built a large room to enjoy dancing. Gertrude kept the home while Chester followed his dreams. He worked hard and rose quickly in his profession. By 1916, he was a qualified draftsman. By 1918, he was an ordinance engineer.

Meanwhile World War I started. The Germans had submarines and America was suffering devastating losses of allied merchant shipping that sometimes reached 800,000 tons per month. Something had to be developed to stop this terrible menace. The Mark I depth charge had been produced in 1917 but as enemy submarines became heavier the explosive charge was not strong enough. The British developed a depth charge but it was neither effective nor safe and was rejected by the United States.

Minkler spent years working to perfect the depth charge that would eventually become effective in igniting a charge in the vicinity of the sub and deliver it a crushing blow. It was called the Mark II and tests were conducted aboard the submarine L-49. It proved safe, transportable, efficient and reliable. In August 1917 he registered his patent in Washington but he assigned all rights, except for commercial ones, to the United States Government thereby forfeiting any royalties to which he was entitled.

England was impressed and adopted it. The U.S. Fleet has used it since the autumn of 1917. The British claim that about 34 German submarines were hit by these depth charges. It helped curtail our shipping losses and contributed to the elimination of the German U-boat from the high seas.

An English firm designed a similar model and attempted to claim patent rights but on October 29, 1929, Minkler was given credit by the Patent Office in Washington. He was recognized as "The father of the depth charge." He never laid claim to the title but his fame as an inventor spread far and wide. He was asked to appear in a film series of the "Master Minds of America." Wanting to avoid publicity, he declined the offer.

Minkler's genius as a designer of torpedoes and other explosives was well known. Secretary of the Navy, Franklin D. Roosevelt, brought him to Washington to aid in developing a torpedo that could be dropped from an airplane.

During the 1930s, he continued to develop and patent various mechanisms that were to prove useful in anti-submarine warfare during World War II. One, which he patented in 1933, was declared top secret. This classification would not be released until 1946, a year after World War II ended.

Chester Minkler retired on July 10, 1942, after 44 years of service. He was 60 years of age. Tributes came from all over the world. For the next three years he worked only one day a week as an unpaid consultant to the Government. His remaining years were spent in this little house where he and Gertrude lived quietly and he puttered in his basement workshop. They had no children. Gertrude died in 1963. Two years later he sold this home and moved to an apartment at 8 Everett Street where he died at the age of 89 on May 18, 1972.

His contribution to both World Wars was impressive. He never sought fame or reward for himself. Self-educated and with Yankee ingenuity he proved that the life and work of an ordinary man can have a vast impact on world history.

The Newport Torpedo Station on Goat Island, ca 1930
Courtesy of the Newport Historical Society

This model of a Mark 14 torpedo was made by William Nimmo, Sr. circa 1946.

The Wissahickon, Bayside Avenue

In the middle of the 18th century, a large portion of land on the Point section belonged to the Hunter family. It extended from the railroad tracks to the water and from Battery Street on northward. Many wealthy people came from the large cities to enjoy the fabulous Newport climate. Among these was Robert I. Maitland. So enamored was he with the land fronting the inner bay of Newport Harbor that he purchased a large portion of this land from Charles Hunter on March 6, 1852. On this land he built a mansion.

Moving the Wissahickon
Courtesy of the Newport Historical Society

The mansion was both beautiful and spacious. It was three stories high with a mansard roof and a cupola that rose one and a half stories higher. The mansion itself stood on what are now the grounds of the Naval Hospital. Lawns, trees, gardens and orchards stretched all the way to Battery Street, while a large well-designed driveway circled to the entrance from Third Street.

On the day of the purchase, Mr. Maitland sold two of the lots at Washington, Battery and Second Street to John Auchincloss. He built his own mansion on land where the Corpus Christi Convent (formerly the Cenacle) now stands. How beautiful these two mansions must have been.

On February 21, 1870, the Maitland mansion was sold to Daniel T. Swinburne, a descendent of the Newport Arnolds and Tews. He, too, loved the sea as did his ancestors and his home became a haven for many scholars, both naval and literary.

In 1909, the heirs of Daniel Swinburne sold the property north of Cypress Street to the United States Government for the sum of $21,700.60 so that the U.S. Naval Hospital could be built. This beautiful house was then moved to the corner of Bayside and Sycamore Streets and placed in a catty-corner position. Slowly the house deteriorated. World War I changed the face of the Point. The Depression changed it even further. This unique home became a rooming and/or boarding house. Like the Plymouth House, its occupants were temporary residents such as actors and actresses. World War II changed it even further.

Purchased by Samuel Gillison in 1941, it was then transformed into an apartment house. It was home to many families and was known throughout the Point as the "Wissahickon." These families also moved on and the building slowly deteriorated. In its later disreputable state, it was a frightening place to many of the Point children.

One Point Hummer tells of his experience as a youth when he and his companions, all about seven or eight years of age, were playing around the grounds and decided to see what was in the "haunted house." A door was open in the basement and they slowly entered. "We were unaware that a medical doctor had once occupied one of the tenements. The light coming through the windows on the water-side of the house was just right for us to see skulls and what we thought were skeletons hanging there. We cleared the area in great haste and never, ever went back."

The once beautiful house was allowed to deteriorate and eventually became a casualty of progress. The building was torn down in the 1960s when the Newport Bridge changed the face of the lovely neighborhood where it once stood. Operation Clapboard and the Old Port Association had not yet been formed. Had they been, this unique and beautiful structure possibly would have been saved, moved again to another location and restored.

The Chapel By The Sea, U.S. Naval Hospital Grounds

This chapel is on the grounds of the Naval Hospital. The hospital was a bustling complex during World War II. It was here that our war casualties were brought or when accidents at sea occurred. Understaffed and overcrowded during the war years, it performed a service for the many Navy men and their families that will always be gratefully remembered.

At the southwestern end of the hospital grounds stands a little white church, "The Chapel by the Sea." It is known to every Point Hummer and to many others throughout the world. Although it was a Naval Chapel, it was always open to the public. The Point Hummers and other Newporters attended the masses there every Sunday and Holy day be they Roman Catholic, Episcopalian, Methodist, Presbyterian, etc. Each denomination had a religious service scheduled at a different time.

Navy men frequently married their brides in this tiny chapel. It is a beautiful site at the water's edge and when the sun sets, it makes you appreciate the beauties of nature. It certainly brought comfort to the many men who were patients at the hospital, especially during the war years. Their families also found comfort sitting on the benches beside the chapel and in front of the hospital gazing at lovely Narragansett Bay.

The chapel still holds services but they have been minimized since the hospital, due to Navy cutbacks, is now manned only by a skeleton staff. However, weddings, christenings and services are still ongoing events there.

The Chapel by the Sea will always live in the memory of anyone who ever visited it. However, sad to say, this lovely Chapel will soon be demolished due to the presence of lead paint and the government regulations concerning its dangers. It will be very sad to see this beautiful building razed.

Van Zandt Pier, Washington Street

As we leave the Chapel by the Sea and begin our walk along the Washington Street waterfront, we come to Van Zandt Pier where thousands of children have learned to swim. Where families gathered on hot summer nights to enjoy the cool breezes and watch the fireworks displays.

The original pier was destroyed during the 1938 hurricane but was rebuilt, destroyed again by a later hurricane, and once again rebuilt. The last destruction forever removed the wooden structure from which many a daring youngster dove from its top into the bay. This structure was never replaced because the city fathers firmly believed that too many large boulders from the original pier lay unseen beneath the waters and the chances were great that an unsuspecting young swimmer might encounter grave danger if diving from too high a point.

This pier could tell many stories. On July 4th, people from all over line the pier to watch the fireworks that light the sky and the bay from Fort Adams or King's Park.

Here the Point Hummers have gathered to swim and chat. Here a young girl chose to end her life. Here, on several occasions the ashes of former Point Hummers were distributed over the waters, as friends and family stood and reminisced about the happy times they shared. Here many a Point Hummer went to cry in solitude when life was troubled. A recent incident was a gentleman who came from out of state to walk on the pier where his mother spent so many happy hours of her youth.

The pier was deteriorating due to the lack of city funding by the city. However, "The Friends of Van Zandt Pier" have formed an association to repair and restore it. These Point Hummers who, as children, grew up in the Point have cherished memories of their happy pier days and want others to enjoy what they were privileged to have, as were their parents before them.

Home of the Artist, Ade de Bethune, 118 Washington Street

This attractive home, between Van Zandt pier and Battery Park, gazes out into Narragansett Bay. It stands alone, with parks on either side of it.

All the land in the area north and east of Battery Park was originally part of the William Dyre property. All of the Dyre property eventually came into the hands of Charles Hunter who laid it out in lots and streets. Robert Maitland purchased a huge tract of this waterfront property. On the day of the sale, he

sold part of it to John Auchincloss. Both men built mansions on their properties.

This particular site was part of the Auchincloss estate and was purchased by George E. Sage. He was a former Navy man who lost his home in the 1906 earthquake and fire in California. Vowing to move as far away from California and never to return there, he piled whatever he could salvage of his furnishings and put them aboard a barge and brought them to Newport. This was before the days of the Panama Canal so it was quite a trip.

Designed in 1906 by the J. Lovett Little Architectural firm of Boston, it was home for many years to Mr. and Mrs. Sage. There have been changes in the original structure. In 1913, the porch was enclosed and the bedroom on the second floor extended over it.

A chauffeur and Chinese servants were employed. The Chinese servants baked cookies for the neighborhood children who were at first frightened by members of a different culture but who soon grew to accept them.

From August 1935 until 1951 it was home to Mr. and Mrs. Frank Sadler. Upon Mrs. Sadler's death the property went into a life estate for her husband and eventually passed on to their son. The years 1951 until 1953 found a new owner occupying this charming home. She was Sarah C. Hazard Peaslee.

It is now the home of Ade de Bethune who was born in Brussels, Belgium in 1914. She was a child when Germany marched in and occupied her country.

Ade's parents were of Belgian aristocracy. Her father, Baron Gaston de Bethune, a chemical engineer and inventor, served under King Albert during World War I. Her mother, Marthe, served her country as an observer, crossing Belgian lines into Holland and England and served time in prison. A great many women participated in these activities to assist their country.

After resigning his commission in the Army, Gaston de Bethune came to the United States to attempt to patent his inventions. The family followed him to New York in August 1928. Here, in 1934, Ade became an illustrator for the Catholic Worker and began her liturgical art career. This brought her to Newport where she studied and worked under the renowned stonecutter John Howard Benson.

In 1940, Ade purchased a colonial home for her parents at 36 Thames Street and they joined her in Newport the following year. In 1947, Marthe de Bethune's father died. When his estate was settled in 1953, with her inheritance she was able to purchase the Washington Street property at a sealed auction and the family moved into it. It has remained in the family for almost 50 years. Ade's studio is on the second floor and the view is magnificent. On the side of her front door is a blue and white tile in honor of St. Leo the Great made by the Rev. Mark Malone, a former pupil of Ade's.

In 1966, Baron de Bethune died at home at the age of 89. He was buried at his request, not embalmed, in a casket of plain pine. He was waked in this home among family and friends. The following day these friends carried the coffin by its rope handles to the church and then to the cemetery in the family station wagon.

Mrs. de Bethune lived in the house until January 5, 1978, when she died at the age of 96. Her funeral, like her husband's, was simple. She was not embalmed and dressed in ordinary clothes with a shawl around her shoulders. She also had a plain coffin.

Today in the hallway of Ade's home is an ordinary hope chest that Ade made herself in 1942 and in which she will eventually be laid to rest. On it are painted the various houses in which she has lived, a set of double doors that personifies the Gate of Heaven, a jeweled cross and a throne.

Ade is known as "The Mother of American Liturgical Art." Not only an artist, she has achieved the distinction of being a humanitarian. A devout Roman Catholic, her cultural background has enhanced a lifetime that has been dedicated not only to her liturgical art but also to the art of helping others.

This house has always been the last one on the waterside. When the street was a dead end, a large house, the Rice estate, blocked Washington Street just north of the Bethune house. When it was decided to extend Washington Street, the road was designed to curve around the Rice property that in later years became the Corpus Christi Convent property. Many years later, the Rice house was moved and attached to the Corpus Christi building on Battery Street.

Liturgical Art by Ade de Bethune

I saw the Holy City, the new Jerusalem...
Revelation 21:2

Creation
In Wisdom hast Thou made all Things
Psalms 104:24

Corpus Christi Convent, Battery Street

John Auchincloss, a New York businessman who summered here with his family, that included nine children, built this house in 1810 and it was his home until 1876. This property and the adjoining Rice estate had piers that extended out into the harbor since both properties enjoyed what is known as riparian rights. These two piers have long since been demolished.

In 1905, the property was transferred from the heirs of John Auchincloss to Agnes Storer and Marie Cisneros for one dollar. The deed stated that the old house was to be removed from the property by William Manuel by November 1905. Miss Storer and her father, Dr Horatio Robinson Storer, invited a small group of nuns from France to come to Newport. They settled on the property in temporary quarters. In 1907, the new convent, that was also a questhouse for affluent Catholic women, was built. The present chapel and Chaplain's residence was added in 1914.

The following year Miss Storer deeded the property to St. Regis Corporation and a Newport Catholic Retreat Center was established known to Newporters as "The Cenacle." It then acquired the adjoining Rathbone-Rice estate.

At this point in time Washington Street was a dead end at the site of the Rice estate. After the end of World War I, the City of Newport opened this road and extended it as an "Esplanade" to the Naval Hospital grounds. At that time the waterfront rights were taken away from the property owners. However, the Cenacle was allowed to retain the small triangular parcel next to the Bethune home.

In 1955, the Corpus Christi Carmelite sisters from Trinidad purchased the property from the St. Regis Corporation, so that they could continue with their retreats and educational work. The nuns had the building enlarged and improved, not for their comfort, but for the guests or "retreatants" as they were called.

73

Children as well as adults have participated in the activities at the Cenacle since the early 1900s. The children attended classes and were instructed not only in religious instruction but also in sewing and other crafts. Women, not only from Newport, but also from other states and countries participated in the retreats that were held where they could contemplate their lives and study and learn.

Services were held in the little chapel where neighbors attended Mass, along with the nuns and retreatants. The Cenacle belonged to the Point and the people belonged to the Cenacle. It was a wonderful time where all joined in to host the many bazaars and activities whose proceeds aided the nuns. The neighborhood boys served as altar boys at all the masses. A chaplain was always in residence.

In 1964, the building on the former Rice estate was moved and connected to the main building and the site became a parking lot for The Cenacle. Sometime after 1964, Corpus Christi donated to the City of Newport a small plot of land across the street and gave up its waterfront rights. This park is now known as the John Martins Park.

Time changes all things. There was another small chapel on the Point, the Naval Chapel that is described in another section. This also served the Newport residents. Many of the Catholic residents of the Point, and other parts of the town, chose to attend the services at one of these two chapels. This left their parishes without their weekly seat fees and budget collection. This did not meet with the approval of the Diocese of Providence. Consequently, both chapels were notified that parishioners were required to attend and support their own church. The Cenacle then curtailed their open door policy. The Navy Chapel did not close to the public, but they too encouraged parishioners to attend their own parish church.

Slowly the Cenacle felt the revolution of the Sixties and the falling away from religion by the young. The Church attempted to bring Catholicism into the modern world, and in doing so most of the old Catholic culture was destroyed. Many missed the Latin liturgy and resented the changes. The clergy and nuns were defecting from the church and the seminaries were half empty. The young boys who served at the masses lost interest. Only 50 percent of those who ordinarily attended Sunday mass continued to do so. Donations were cut in half. Catholic schools were closing. Churches closed their doors during the day because of vandalism. Vigil candles were not allowed to burn until they finally extinguished themselves. The insurance companies felt they were a fire hazard.

So time changed things and it was not for the better. The financial situation had no solution. The Cenacle closed its doors about 1991. The nuns left the Cenacle building and moved into a small residential home in the area. In the intervening years the closed buildings and grounds have deteriorated.

In 1996, the Rhode Island Housing and Mortgage Finance Corporation purchased the property from Corpus Christi. For almost four years efforts have been made by "The Star of the Sea" organization to obtain financing and zoning to turn this neglected property into a retirement home, restoring its former beauty and making it again a jewel on the Point.

Ade Bethune's dream of renovating the former convent into senior housing may be coming closer to reality. At an April 2000 press conference, attended by U.S. Rep. Patrick Kennedy and other city officials, it was announced that Star of the Sea had received approval of a $4.6 million finance package from Rhode Island Housing. "Harbor Point", the name of the congregate living facility, will offer a combination of one-bedroom and efficiency units for people 62 and older. No two apartments will be alike and common areas will include a library, solarium, decks and gardens.

The United States Department of the Interior believes that the Corpus Christi chapel built in 1914 is a significant historical building and must be preserved. It's natural acoustic quality reflects and enhances the human voice. Another noteworthy feature of this chapel is the set of 9 double lancet stained glass memorial windows that are the work of Joseph Gardiner Reynolds, circa 1920.

Battery Park (The Blue Rocks), Washington St.

Next to the de Bethune home is a semi-circular expanse that commands a spectacular view of the bay and the mouth of the Atlantic Ocean. This spot is known as Battery Park and formerly as Fort Greene. It has always been a part of all who lived on the Point. It was the site where all public baptisms of the Baptist Church were performed in the mid 17th century. Candidates would be immersed in the chilly waters of the bay on rocks called the "Blue Rocks."

Before the Revolutionary War there were four houses on this section of land. In April of 1776, the neighborhood became vital to the safety of the residents of the Point. On August 27, 1799, President John Adams purchased the site of the North Battery. Three houses were then torn down to afford a suitable location for the erection of the fort. It was built in semi-circular form, with a breastwork containing twelve guns. The house of Mrs. Mary Wing was left standing and enclosed. The British later tore this down in 1783. Fort Greene was named in honor of General Nathaniel Greene and it would remain U.S. Government property until 1926.

The British sloop of war "The Scarborough" put into Newport harbor during the war. On her deck were 20 guns and 245 men. A garrison of 150 men was stationed at the fort and they were ready to defend the town in case of invasion. She was met with a fiery greeting from the battery of guns aimed at her from the shore.

When Fort Adams was built, Fort Greene was abandoned. In 1887, Congress authorized the City of Newport to use Fort Greene solely as a park and at this time the fort was filled in and made into a park known as Battery Park. On June 1926, the War Department announced the proposed sale of the fort. At an auction on July 2, 1926, with other bidders withdrawing in deference to the city's offer, the tract was purchased for $5,471.41. On September 30, 1926, Mayor Garreston presented it to the City of Newport to be forever preserved as a public park.

Today, the outer wall is the only visible part of the fort that lies buried intact beneath the soil and grass of the park. One can follow the faint indentation of half circles where the park has settled. This outlines the battery where the twelve guns were mounted, in pairs, turned to defend the fort and the harbor.

In later years before TV entered our lives, the summer evenings would see the park crowded with most of the local Point Hummers. Men swapped stories while sitting on the benches. Women brought the children to play and wade in the waters of the shore. A bandstand stood in the center and a snack

stand to the side. A band played music almost every evening.

Today, although not crowded as in bygone days, it is still one of Newport's most loved spots. Now there are no crowds. However, walkers from all over the island and from out of town, find peace, quiet and cool breezes away from the TV world

It is a beautiful sight to watch the sun set over the bay at the end of the day. Ironically, nowadays people vie for parking spaces along the edge of the park and many sit in their cars just enjoying the view and the cooling breezes. Others, however, walk along the same waterfront street and sit on the restored benches, many now bearing a plaque with the name of a former Point Hummer. Most are enjoying the same smells and sounds they did when their parents brought them there as children many years ago.

In 1949, a young Navy veteran, who was born in Newport, sat and watched a storm approaching and wrote the following poem.

The Coming of the Storm
as seen from the Blue Rocks, Newport, R.I.

The air was crisp and clean
And grass was wet with dew;
As clouds began to screen
The sun's rays from our view.
While seagulls flew inland
A sign of storm at sea;
The pounding surf on sand
Warned all in sight to flee.
White caps seemed to protest
The sudden change in scene;
Came angrily to rest
In waves no more serene.
All nature was aware
By it's instinctive law;
That soon the storm would share
The beauty that we saw.

Carlo Lozito 1949

Mr. Lozito now resides in California

Stella Maris Convent, 91 Washington Street

This land was a part of the land granted to the Eastons when Newport was partitioned. When Nicholas Easton died, his widow gave this parcel of land to the Society of Friends. In the early 1800s, Edward Mayer left Austria and came to New York where he became very successful. He married Agatha Minturn the tenth of eleven children of Esther (Robinson) and James Minturn. Esther was related to Quaker Tom Robinson. This is probably the reason why Edward Mayer came to Newport. The Mayers had three children, John, Lloyd and William.

Mr. Mayer purchased the lots on the waterside and also purchased two lots across the street that extended to Second Street. On these lots he commissioned George Burroughs to build for Mrs. Mayer a magnificent stone house that was called "Blue Rocks." In 1853, the Overseers of the R.I. Society of Friends conveyed to Agatha Mayer the lot on which Ft. Greene stands. This was considered a rental since the fort itself remained government property. So the Mayer property extended from Cherry Street to Battery Street and from the harbor to Second Street. It contained a greenhouse and gardens. On the waterside property another garden was created with winding paths, at the end of which was a pier. Stone was brought from Portland, Conn., for the mansion. The inside was finished with black walnut. It was completed in 1861.

One summer night, in 1874, Agatha Minturn Mayer, melancholy and depressed, felt the spirits calling her. She walked through the garden to the end of the pier where she threw herself into the water. Her sister Frances was married to Thomas Hazard who was a spiritualist and the owner of a beautiful home called "Vaucluse." On this estate he built a wing to house the spirits that he felt were always present. It was felt at the time that perhaps he influenced Agatha.

The Mayer children kept the property and rented it until 1893. Lloyd Mayer, the second son of

Edward and Agatha, sold the property in 1896 to Frederick Cunningham from Massachusetts who spent summers here for ten years. The mansion was then rented as a summer residence until 1922 when Irma Wetheravill Parish purchased it.

Agnes Storer, a Washington Street resident, then purchased the property. It became a convalescent home for the affluent under the management of the Sisters of Cluny. The little house across the street became their convent. The nuns renamed the mansion, formerly known as "Blue Rocks" to "Stella Maris... Star of the Sea." In September of 1942, the ownership was transferred to the R.I. Roman Catholic Diocese by the will of Agnes Storer.

The two parcels next to the little house where the nuns lived were vacant lots surrounded by high shrubs. On hot summer days the nuns would venture into this area in long swimming suits and enjoyed their own privacy while swimming in the bay.

In 1982, the nuns left and the Stella Maris was closed. In 1965, the Diocese sold the little house on the waterside, still known as "Blue Rocks." to Hiram and Caroline Stout. Three years later Edward and Ingrid Beach purchased it and finally, in June of 1972, Dr. Charles Shoemaker and his wife Stephanie became the owners.

In 1987, the mansion, together with the two remaining lots across the street, became the property of the Stella Maris Development Corporation. Records show the purchase price to be $1,800,000.

In 1989, the Maddens purchased and completely renovated it. In 1990, they opened it as a Bed and Breakfast Inn. It is now listed under the National Register of Historic Places.

The lots on the waterside were developed into four high-priced condominiums. During the construction, the developers went into bankruptcy and the condominiums were sold unfinished.

The Beehive House, 88 Washington Street

In 1915, Julia Belnap purchased the land between Chestnut and Cherry Streets on the waterside from the Fairchild family. This property consisted of two lots. On the northern lot was a large Victorian house. It was a lovely house and had a wrap-around porch on three sides. The entire property was sold for $11,095.82. From its description and location this could very well have been the house where Bret Harte wrote "A Newport Romance."

Where the Beehive house now stands was a large copper beach tree, which probably came down during the 1938 hurricane. The house and the lot on the north side were sold in June 1951 to Dorothy Tuckerman Draper and eventually to the Mayor Henry Wheeler and his wife. The Wheelers demolished the old house in 1941 and built the one that now stands at 94 Washington Street.

Admiral and Mrs. Belnap sold the lot on the south side to Agnes Storer. In time, John Howard Benson and his wife purchased the land and were preparing to build when Mrs. Benson's father died and his home at 62 Washington Street became theirs. The Belnap property then changed hands again. First it was sold to Mr. and Mrs. Powel Kazanjian, who decided not to build there, and then to David Feltham.

David Feltham enlarged it by bringing in a barge and anchoring it to the property, then filling the land in with whatever materials he could obtain. This brought a storm of protests from the Pointers and eventually, discouraged by the complaints and the hard work, vowing that he would never sell it to Newporters, he sold the property to Charles and Anne Reynolds of Worcester, Mass.

With tremendous foresight, for the restoration of colonial homes was in its infancy, Mr. and Mrs. Reynolds located the John Tripp House that was built about 1725 and about to be demolished. A one-story gambrel with a partly exposed chimney of brick and stone, it originally stood on Manton Avenue in Providence, R.I. The Reynolds purchased the house. In 1965, friends of the Reynolds assisted in the dismantling, labeling every beam and post, then trucked the disassembled house to Newport, where it was reconstructed on the foundation that had been prepared for it. It was placed with the end to the sidewalk. In 1972, the owner's son added an addition.

This adorable house, nestled in this quiet neighborhood, seems as if it has always been here.

Aubois House, 86 Washington Street

Mr. and Mrs. Guy Norman possibly built this house. It is known that they raised the former small house up one story, added to it and covered it with stucco so that it was quite different. They lived in it for over thirty years.

Mrs. Norman was the former Louise Palfrey of Boston, a summer colonist who preferred to live on the

Point rather than on Bellevue Avenue. However, she did maintain a staff of servants while she lived in this home. Mr. Norman died comparatively young during World War I.

In the spring of 1940, Mr. and Mrs. Eugene O'Reilly purchased it. Since they had a large family with many young children, they feared for their safety so close to the water. The heavy traffic that the waterfront street bore during World War II was also a concern.

Therefore they moved and rented the home. A young Naval officer was supposedly the tenant. However, this young man was quite a hero. During the war, he parachuted into Italy to bring out a team of Italian men (consisting of an Admiral, two captains, four engineers and five technicians) who disagreed with Mussolini. These men were brought to Newport to assist with the development of a magnetic torpedo exploder that the Italians knew much more about than the Americans.

The men resided in this home during the war and a young Newport girl was hired to teach them English. Margharita Russo was later to marry Alfredo Sciarrotta, one of her Italian pupils. They would remain in Newport after the war and he would later become one of Newport's leading silversmiths.

The house has been the home of Mrs. Suzanne Aubois for many years.

Weaver Cottage, 19 Chestnut Street

This charming cottage, which stands on the corner of Chestnut and Washington Streets, was built by George and Eleanor Weaver in 1976-77. The 17th and 18th Century materials used were collected over many years and consisted of gunstock beams, ceiling beams, wide floor boards, doors, hardware, etc. The chimney and fireplace bricks, also 18th Century, were cleaned and reused.

The chimney is a copy of a 17th Century chimney. The addition at the rear of the building was added in the year 1995. While this material is new, all details such as the cornices, moldings, etc., were copied to match the main house.

George Weaver, a descendant of the early settlers, knew the heritage of Newport and understood the construction of its colonial buildings. When Doris Duke started her restoration of Newport, he accepted the position as assistant to Mr. Francis Comstock, the Director of the Newport Restoration Foundation and worked for many years in that position. He also worked in the private renovation of many of the Newport homes.

Although Mr. and Mrs. Weaver restored many other homes that they themselves owned, this one was the one they built for their retirement. His knowledge is evident in every feature of this home. It is a home built with love and pride. Every beam, every brick, and every window was carefully planned. Certainly it is a tribute to his memory.

It is the residence of Mrs. George Duncan Weaver.

Weaver Cottage Family Room

The Villa Marina, 72 Washington Street

In 1859, a millionaire named Milton Sanford came to Newport from Massachusetts. He purchased John Goddard's house and shop on the corner of Willow and Washington Street on the driftway side. He also purchased the Easton house on the north side of Goddard's. The Goddard house was then moved to Second Street and his shop to Smith Court.

On these two lots, Mr. Sanford erected his mansion. It is a Victorian Tudor designed by Architect William Ralph Emerson and built in 1870. He named it the "Villa Edna." He and Mrs. Sanford entertained a distinguished circle of friends here. It is a beautiful house with a large wrap-around porch overlooking the bay.

The Sanfords had no children and when they died, the property went to two of Mr. Sanford's nieces. Later the house was sold to William King Covell at auction in 1895. It was stipulated in the deed that the name "Villa Edna" no longer be used, so the name was changed to "Villa Marina." The Wm. King Covell family had resided for almost 50 years at 43 Farewell Street. When they purchased the waterfront home, they found the winters exceptionally chilly and retreated to the home on Farewell Street during the cold months. Later the home was winterized and occupied year round.

The grandson of William King Covell lived in this house for many years. He was known as "King" and while he lived the house was always known as the "King Covell House." The passing years have changed that and it is again known as the "Villa Marina."

Many personages have relaxed on the porch of this gracious home finding peace and tranquility.

Among the most famous, or infamous, were Bret Harte, noted author, and Lizzie Borden who was accused of murdering her father and stepmother. Lizzie was found innocent but notoriety followed her all her life.

She wrote to Sarah Remington Covell, an old friend, requesting to spend time in Newport. Sarah gladly obliged and Lizzie came to Newport for a few weeks to relax. As a "thank you" gift, she sent Mrs. Covell a set of sterling silver pie forks that are still in use by the family. George Bancroft, former Secretary of the Navy and founder of the Naval Academy, once owned the dining room set presently in the house.

Kate Fields, the well-known artist, was the niece of Mrs. Sanford. One of the bedrooms is named after her. Upon the death of "King" Covell, the house was deeded to the Society for the Preservation of New England Antiquities. A provision in the deed gave Covell family members first right of refusal should the Society sell the property. Funds to repair and maintain the house were scarce so the Society had to relinquish ownership. Richard and Anne Cuvelier, the daughter of Elizabeth Covell Ramsey, reacquired the property on behalf of the Covell family.

They have done tremendous rehabilitation work on this elegant mansion. Its beautiful foyer rises three stories to the roof with lovely frescoes, carved woodwork and indoor balconies. A wraparound porch overlooks a large inground swimming pool. The magnificent view of Narragansett Bay from this house is unsurpassed.

Bret Harte

Bret(t) Harte, American short story writer, novelist and poet (1836-1902) was born in Albany, NY. When he was 19 years of age, he went to California where he mined gold and taught school before he became a journalist. It was in California that his stories were born. His work was sentimental. This was the land of shacks, ditches, crumbling roads, bars and gangs of bullies.

What made his work so important was that he wrote about real people. The schoolmistress, the sheriff and his posse, the bad man, the gambler, the harlot with a heart of gold were individuals he had known. Sometimes Harte revealed their true backgrounds in Virginia, Kentucky or New England.

His work was sentimental. He portrayed thieves, vagabonds and miners as more admirable than conventional, law-abiding folks. He showed the goodness in the heart of the outcasts.

In 1871, he returned East but never found the earlier appeal of his imagination. He eventually settled in England where he spent the rest of his life, the leader of a literary circle of writers who had left America.

In the late 1860s, he wrote his best-remembered pieces. During that time he visited Newport often as a friend of the well-known Kate Fields, the niece of Milton Sanford of Villa Edna. It was in Newport that he wrote "A Newport Romance."

Bret Harte wrote this poem in 1880. The house is described but not identified. It is definitely on Washington Street. It is evidently a large house with a long veranda and is next to the water. It has a library, gaslights line the street, and it is near a fort. Within a neighbor's house a dance is in progress and the dancers swing to a waltz.

A Newport Romance.

They say that she died of a broken heart
(I tell the tale as it was told to me),
But her spirit lives, and her soul is part
Of this sad old house by the sea.

Her lover was fickle and fine and French.
It was nearly a hundred years ago
When he sailed away from her arms — poor wench —
With the Admiral Rochambeau.

87

I marvel much what periwigged phrase
Won the heart of this sentimental Quaker
At what golden-laced speech of those modish days
She listened — the mischief take her.

But she kept the posies of mignonette
That he gave and ever as their bloom failed
And faded (though with her tears still wet)
Her youth with their own exhaled.

Till one night, when the sea-fog wrapped a shroud
Round spar and spire and tarn and tree,
Her soul went up on that lifted cloud
From the sad old house by the sea.

And ever since then, when the clock strikes two,
She walks unbidden from room to room
And the air is filled as she passes through
With a subtle, sad perfume.

The delicate odor of mignonette,
The ghost of a dead and gone bouquet,
Is all that tells of her story, yet
Could she think of a sweeter way?

I sit in the sad old house tonight —
Myself a ghost from a farther sea:
And I trust that this Quaker woman might,
In courtesy, visit me.

For the laugh is fled from porch and lawn,
And the bugle died from the fort on the hill
And the twitter of girls on the stairs is gone
And the grand piano is stilled.

Somewhere in the darkness a clock strikes two,
And there is no sound in the sad old house,
But the long veranda dripping with dew
And in the wainscot a mouse.

The light in my study-lamp streams out
From the library door — but has gone astray
In the depths of the darkened hall. Small doubt
But the Quakeress knows the way.

Was it a trick of a sense o'erwrought
With outward watching and inward fret?
But I swear that the air just now was fraught
With the odor of mignonette.

I open the window — and seem almost —
So still lies the ocean — to hear the beat
Of its Great Gulf artery off the coast,
And to bask in its tropic heat.

In my neighbor's windows the gas-lights flare
As the dancers swing in a waltz of Strauss
And I wonder now could I fit that air
To the song of this sad old house.

And no odor of mignonette there is
But the breath of morn on the dewey lawn
And mayhap from causes as slight as this
The quaint old legend is born.

But the soul of that subtle, sad perfume,
As the spiced embalmings, they say, outlast
The mummy laid in his rocky tomb,
Awakens my buried past.

And I think of the passion that shook my youth
Of its aimless loves and its idle pains,
And I'm thankful now for the certain truth
That only the sweet remains.

And I hear no rustle of stiff brocade,
And I see no face at the library door
For now that the ghosts of my heart are laid
She is viewless for evermore

But whether she came as a faint perfume
Or whether a spirit in stole of white,
I feel, as I pass from the darkened room
She has been with my soul tonight.

St. John the Evangelist Church, Washington Street

Situated among the colonial houses on the Point is the Church of St. John the Evangelist, an Episcopal/Anglican church. Every day the bells of Saint John's ring out marking the hours from early morning until evening. They ring also for other occasions, calling the faithful to prayer, weddings, funerals, and other important events. For each service the chimes ring differently. They speak a message to all.

In 1875, the Rev. Dr. White was the rector of Trinity Church. It was then that he organized a society composed of several young men of the parish that adopted the name of St. Stephen's Guild. It was suggested that the Guild would start a Mission service and would work in that part of the city known as "The Point." This large district had no public place of worship and therefore many in the area never attended church.

The Guild's first service was held in a little house on Third and Poplar Street on July 11, 1875, in the home of Peter Quire. This man was the son of freed slaves and a member of Trinity Church. Mr. Quire was born in Baltimore in 1806. He came to Newport from Philadelphia where living the life of a free black person was far worse than that of a slave in the South. Mr. Quire graciously offered the sitting room in his home for the services and his wife made sure the room was always clean and in order for the services.

For the first service, the room was filled. Interest increased steadily and it soon became evident that larger accommodations would have to be found. It was decided to erect a building, since there were no large rooms or public buildings available in that part of the city. A lot was found on Poplar Street and subscriptions were secured. The city defrayed part of the expense of the tower so that the bell could also be used as a fire alarm. An attractive building known as the Guild Hall was in the process of being completed.

Suddenly Dr. White died from a bad cold. The new bell tolled for the pastor's death before a service had ever been held in the building. However, the building continued. Dr. White had chosen the altar. Furniture and gifts poured in. The Free Chapel of St. John the Evangelist was ready and the first service was held on February 13, 1876. The crowd was so large that many had to be turned away. This was to be their home until 1894.

Easter of 1876 found a new rector at Trinity. The Rev. George Magill took an interest in the new chapel and held a weekly evening service there. Dr. White's widow would not let her husband's project fail and she started a Sunday school that began with six to eight children and this group grew to one hundred and fifty. She moved to the Point where her friends purchased a cottage for her with a piazza and French roof on the corner of Poplar and Second Street. She wanted to be close to the Chapel that was more of a monument to her husband Isaac than Trinity Church could ever have been.

In 1883, St. John's had 100 communicants. The first funeral to be held in the chapel was that of Harriet Hazard Quire (wife of Peter). The first wedding was of Capt. E.O. Matthews, USN and his bride Harriet. Sadly, hers was the second of the funerals.

In 1887, the parish had many problems and they worsened. The year 1889 was one of depression and discouragement for the parish. It appeared that they no longer could continue as an independent organization. Warden Wilfred Eddy presented a petition for the purpose of reuniting with Trinity Church as a Mission Chapel once again. It was carried by a vote of 7-2. There had been nothing but deficits since 1882. Their pastor, Fr. Moran resigned. Both he and the pastor before him had worked hard to raise money so that the Chapel could be independent but the maintenance problems were overwhelming. The tasks were too great for them. However, during this time the Bishop put off acting on the resolution to rejoin Trinity Church.

Friendship is very important in times of crisis. Wealthy friends, both rich and prominent, can mean a lot. Sarah Titus Zabriskie, daughter of Sarah Jane Titus Zabriskie of Newport, was such a friend. The younger Sarah married Dr. Frank Jackson and had a daughter Ethel, but the marriage failed and divorce was not countenanced either by family or church. Further, young Sarah took back her maiden name. The elder Sarah was saddened by these events. Ostracism by Newport Society was not desirable. However, a generous contribution to the church could accomplish wonders in any society. Sarah Jane Titus Zabriskie died in 1892, leaving her daughter a great deal of money. In March 1893, the young Sarah Zabriskie announced that she would be very happy to build a new church for St. John's parish. Her offer was gratefully accepted.

Land was purchased from the Benjamin Smith estate on Washington and Willow Streets. In September 1893, the cornerstone was laid with a large crowd gathered at the site. A copper box with the date inscribed was placed in the stone. Inside the box were a Bible, a Book of Common Prayer, a copy of the history of the Church and some coins of the year 1893. Although all the other materials may disintegrate with time, the coins will endure.

In November 1894, the church was finished and consecrated as the Zabriskie Memorial Church of St. John the Evangelist. Sarah Zabriskie and her brother, Andrew Christian Zabriskie, attended. Bishop Clarke stated that in the future all persons approaching from the Harbor would glimpse the new tower and that it would stand until the end of the world.

Peter Quire, pictured on next page, truly the father of the church, died in 1899. He had no children and had lived alone since Harriet died in 1893. When his house was sold, he left half of his estate to the

St. John's endowment fund. This amounted to four hundred and nineteen dollars.

For over a hundred years St. John's has graced the waterfront. Everyone on the Point loves this church. Its doors are open to all as they stroll on Washington Street and each year the Point Fair is held on the grounds and people of all faiths happily join together. Proud and beautiful, St. John's stands facing Narragansett Bay. It is one of the very few churches today whose doors are open daily welcoming all.

Peter Quire
Courtesy of the Newport Historical Society

The John Dennis House, 65 Poplar Street

Captain John Dennis was a notorious person. He was perhaps the most successful privateer of the 18th Century. From 1743 to 1756, he terrorized French and Spanish shipping throughout the West Indies, capturing tons of silver, gold, currency and merchandise. He even captured 223 free Spaniards, selling them into slavery mistaking them for Africans. They were eventually returned after the Governor of Cuba captured some of Dennis' crew.

Dennis built this house in 1740. The "Widow's Walk" on the top of the house was characteristic of many of the waterfront homes. It was designed so that the wives of sailors could look from these rooftops for the first sight of a returning loved one. In 1756, Dennis embarked from Newport on a brand new privateering ship and was never heard from again.

The Dennis house once stood closer to the corner of Washington and Poplar Streets. Benjamin Smith made extensive interior and exterior renovations to it and moved this old house back from the sidewalk.

At that time, doors facing the water were considered to be the front doors of a house. These doors faced the water so their masters could view the wharves, warehouses and ships.

When the Hunter house was being renovated and the door on the waterside widened, the pineapple above the door was discarded and thrown into a dump pile. Rescued by Esther Fisher Benson (sister of Benjamin Smith) it was then placed above the back entrance of the Dennis home. In later years when the Preservation Society restored the Hunter house, they reclaimed the pineapple that was then rein-stalled on the Hunter house, but this time on the Washington Street entrance. A replica was then placed on the Dennis house.

This home is now the Rectory of St. John the Evangelist Church.

Quaker Tom Robinson House, 64 Washington Street

As you walk down the cobblestone streets of the Point, you will discover nameplates on the 18th Century homes that identify each house and tell of its priceless history. The home of Quaker Tom Robinson is one of these. This house is on the waterside of the street and sits on the sidewalk boundary. It is a gracious home with a central double doorway. Flowerpots adorn each side of the doorstep.

It is truly one of the finer homes on the Point. On the front of the house there is a tablet that reads "Home of Quaker Tom Robinson and his descendants from 1759. Headquarters of Le Comte de Noailles 1780-1781." Here Quaker Tom resided with his family. Nearby were the homes of his relatives, also Quakers.

Rowland Robinson, the patriarch of the family, came to the colonies with neither money nor friends. He became a carpenter, worked hard and in time he became very rich. His wife was the daughter of a wealthy farmer and together they raised a large family. He bought large tracts of land from the Indians and built a home around Point Judith, R.I.

Quaker Tom Robinson was his grandson. He was born in 1730, to Rowland's eldest son William. He married Sarah Richardson of Newport where they raised a large family. William T. Robinson was the oldest son and Joseph Jacobs Robinson was the youngest son. Quaker Tom's wife was charming and gracious and his daughters were not only beautiful but also accomplished. He purchased the original home in 1759 and extended it to the north to attain additional space and elegance. It remained the same for many years. In 1872, he turned the original kitchen into a living room overlooking the harbor and added a new kitchen wing to the south of the oldest section of the house. At this point, he also added the porch. He furnished it with pieces designed and built by his neighbor John Goddard. At one

94

time it had its own wharf and shop like the Hunter House.

While the British were in Newport, two or three officers were quartered at many of the Newport homes. These officers were the younger sons of some of England's leading families who were seeking their fortunes in His Majesty's Army. Although not popular with the rebellious colonists, they were certainly glamorous. Some of the Newport girls fell in love with them. Many eloped and married them. Molly Robinson was 19 at this time and her parents were deeply concerned when she appeared to have fallen in love with Capt. Thomas Parkin. Mrs. Robinson sent Molly, her sister and small brother away to their uncle in Narragansett, R.I. They were not permitted to return until the British left the island.

In September 1780, the authorities ordered Quaker Tom to take into his household the Comte de Noailles, brother-in-law of Napoleon, who would use the house as his quarters while the French troops occupied Newport. Mary and her siblings returned at this time but it appears she did not forget Capt. Parkin.

The Comte became very fond of the Robinson family and to his pleasure he found that they spoke fluent French. The family was grateful to the French officers and did everything they could to make them comfortable. When the Comte returned to France, his wife (the sister of Madame de Lafayette) wrote to Mrs. Robinson thanking her for her kindness and sent her an exquisite set of Serves china. This set is not in the house today but is in the possession of a descendent who resides in Philadelphia.

During this time, the younger Robinsons, their friends and the French officers made merry by dancing the evenings away. After the war, Mrs. Robinson corresponded regularly with the Comte and comforted him during the loss of his wife and family to the guillotine during the French Revolution.

When Capt. Parkin left Newport, he joined the British Army in Yorktown, Virginia. In 1782, Molly learned of his death at age 28 at Yorktown. She never mentioned his name in letters until 1812 when she sent a silhouette she had of him, shown at right, to her sister Abigail who was completing a book of silhouettes.

When she was 36, Mary (Molly) Robinson married the banker John Morton, an Irish immigrant. At that time, she left Newport to live with her husband and his family in Philadelphia. She was a beloved mother and grandmother to her children and stepchildren. She died at age 80 in Philadelphia.

After her death, a small lacquer box was found among her possessions containing a prayer book, bits of poetry, several notes and a love letter folded with love knots all dated from 50 years before. Among the items in the box was a notice that read: On the ninth of the tenth month, 1782, departed this life, Thomas Parkin Esq., aged about 28 years. He was an officer of the British army, a native of Yorkshire, England, and was killed by a cannon bullet, at the time of the capture of Lord Cornwallis and the army under his command, at Yorktown in Virginia. She closed the box to the past but never threw its contents away. Many things have changed with time, but the house still stands. The old clock that ticked in the days of the occupation remains in the same place.

In 1860, Benjamin Smith inherited the property. He then purchased three other houses on the corner of Poplar and Washington Streets to prevent a large commercial pier taking these lots. As a result, he saved three colonial houses and one Victorian house from demolition.

In 1931, French warships visited Newport and among the officers was a Duc de Noailles, a descendent of the Comte de Noailles, the officer who had been stationed at the home of the Robinson's. The descendants of the two families were joined together in friendship, as had their ancestors 150 years before.

This house is one of the most beautiful on the Point. It was recently sold to J. Pearsall and W. Doyle.

The Hunter House, 54 Washington Street

The first owner of this land was Nathaniel Sheffield. The property, where the present house stands, was given by Nathaniel to his son James, who sold it to Jonathan Nichols Jr. on April 12, 1748. The property contained a wharf, warehouse and other buildings. None of these are believed to be the present Hunter House. Jonathan Nichols is believed to have built the original house. He was the descendent of an old Welsh family, a prosperous merchant who achieved local prominence when he purchased the property.

He was born in Newport on October 24, 1712, the third generation of his family in Rhode Island. He was married to the former Mary Lawton by whom he had eight children. Mary died shortly after he purchased the property. The house was known as the mansion of hospitality. In addition to having a large farm in Portsmouth, he also owned several ships that plied a lucrative trade along the Atlantic routes. He purchased the land on Easton's Point to accommodate this business. This two-mile strip of harbor front was where merchants, captains, shipbuilders and sail makers had their homes and businesses. His wharf and warehouses contained large supplies of merchandise. At the time of his death he was Deputy Governor of Rhode Island.

After he died in 1754, his brother Benjamin sold the house with its wharf, warehouse and other buildings in 1756. The buyer was Colonel Joseph Wanton, Jr., who paid more than 36,000 pounds. He is believed to have doubled the size of the house.

The second owner of the Hunter house, who also was a Deputy Governor, was born in Newport on

February 8, 1730, the oldest son of Mary and Joseph Winthrop Wanton. His father was a merchant trader and he enjoyed the advantages of his family's wealth and position. He enrolled in Harvard University at the age of 16 and at the age of 26 married Abigail Honyman of Newport. However, Abigail died on May 31, 1771. Four years later Joseph remarried this time to Sarah Brenton also of Newport.

Colonel Wanton was a wealthy merchant and an ardent loyalist. When public sentiment in Newport swung in favor of loyalism, Wanton and his father, then Governor, both enjoyed the power and prestige of public office. The younger Wanton failed in his reelection bid when the colony moved toward revolution in 1774 and was forced to stay at home for fear of reprisals on the streets.

His father was ousted as Governor in 1775 and young Wanton was finally arrested by American troops in Newport on Christmas day in 1775. He was taken before an American Commander to swear allegiance to the Revolutionary cause, which he refused to do. He was placed under guard at his Jamestown, R.I. farm until British forces occupied Newport and he was allowed to return.

Had Britain won her fight to maintain control over the American colonies, Wanton would have become a hero. Fate and valor dictated otherwise. When the British left Newport and the French arrived, Wanton fled the city of his birth and joined the British in New York where he died in 1780. The State of Rhode Island confiscated his splendid home on the Point. His widow and infant son, who remained at home, were left to the mercy of the State Legislature. Thus ended the Wanton dynasty.

On August 10, 1780, when the French Fleet entered Newport harbor, the Newporters welcomed them. Without an enemy at her portals, with the vivacious and fun loving French in the town, Newport again became alive even if only in the shadow of her former prosperity. The Wanton house was dark and Admiral de Ternay, Commander of the French fleet, was ill and asked Rhode Island for the use of it as his residence and headquarters.

Here he died on December 5, 1780. He was laid out in state in a room shrouded in black crepe. The coffin was covered with a beautiful embroidered cloth, upon which was draped the new flag of the Americans. French priests took turns chanting prayers throughout the night.

At the funeral, the priests carried lighted tapers followed by eight sailors carrying the coffin from Washington (then Water) Street to Trinity Churchyard on Spring Street. In the northeast corner of this Church of England graveyard, Roman Catholic rites were performed and the coffin was lowered into the earth that had been privately consecrated. The house remained the quarters for French officers, a vault for the fleet's treasures and a base for French naval supplies until the French left Newport in 1781.

After the war, the house was unoccupied for the most part. It was neglected and allowed to deteriorate. Like Newport it fell on hard times. The wharf and outbuildings became ramshackle. The house, occupied at various times by a succession of tenants, became dilapidated. In 1786, the State finally sold it to absentee owners for 2,700 pounds. It sold again in 1794 and once again in 1795. It was not until 1805 that William Hunter and an associate purchased it at auction for a mere $5,000.

William Hunter, like the previous owners of the house, was a Newport native. Born here on November 26, 1774, he was the youngest of four living children of Dr. William Hunter, a Scottish immigrant physician, and Deborah Malbone, a descendent of the Newport Wantons.

William studied medicine but turned to law and was admitted to the bar in 1795. In 1805, he married Mary Robinson, a Quaker of New York City and a Wanton descendent whose grandfather Quaker Tom Robinson lived on Washington Street. William was an Episcopalian and the Robinson's objections were strong, but the young couple married and did eventually move into the Hunter house where eight of their nine children were born. Only six of the children survived childhood.

Politics interested William Hunter more than law and he began a career in Washington where he and his family moved. This lasted until 1821when he lost his reelection bid. The Hunters remained in the house and lived in genteel poverty until 1834 when Mr. Hunter was appointed by President Andrew Jackson to a position in Brazil and the Hunters left Newport to reside there. As long as he lived in this house it was kept intact. When he left Newport he was unable to sell the house and during their absence the house was leased as a boarding house. The tenants did not take care of the property. It deteriorated and Hunter's son called it "Ricketty Hall." When the Hunters returned to Newport in 1835, they had to occupy other quarters until they could clean and refurbish the home.

Here on December 3, 1849, William Hunter died. Mrs. Hunter remained until 1851 when she again leased the house for $100 a month. She then put the former showcase on the market. It was finally sold in 1853 for $10,000. This was followed by a succession of owners. In 1854, the Old Colony Steamship Company purchased the property and it ceased to be a private residence.

In the 1870s, Dr. Mayer operated a nursing home in the building and the front and back doors were widened. The beautiful pediment over the back door facing the bay was taken down and thrown away. Fortunately a person who appreciated beautiful things found it and it was rescued and for many years adorned the Dennis House. It now once again is in its rightful place, the Hunter House.

The Storer family of Boston, Florida, and Newport purchased the house in 1881. Dr. Storer had intended to use the house as a convalescent home but circumstances prevented this. In 1917, they donated it to St. Joseph's Church for use as a convent. When the convent closed in the early 1940s, it remained unoccupied.

In 1945, although not many people were aware of it, the "Committee of 100" was formed with the idea of purchasing the house. John Howard Benson, a member of the committee, asked George Henry Warren if he would buy the house and save it for Newport and the future. Otherwise, it would be destroyed and the paneled rooms sold and scattered among museums and art dealers.

Mr. Warren had never been in the house but he realized from photographs that he had viewed that the house was an important part of Newport. He agreed to sign a note for the amount necessary. Three other well-established Newport citizens added their signatures. This was done with the provision that no part of the building would ever leave Newport. The house was purchased from St. Joseph's Parish for $15,000. The following year the house was donated to the newly formed Preservation Society of Newport County that would restore it and open it to the public.

The Hunter House today is considered to be one of the ten finest colonial period homes in existence in America. It is resplendent with Townsend and Goddard furniture, along with the silver, china and paintings by Newport's finest craftsmen and artists. This superb collection has been acquired for display thanks to the generosity of many. Some of it has been returned from as far away as Scotland. The Preservation Society now opens the house to guided tours so that all who desire may see how prosperous Newport merchants lived before the Revolution.

Pictured below is the Jacob Rodriguez Rivera House that once stood in close proximity to the Hunter House. It was known as the house with a thousand windows.

The Point has changed little since the Nichols, the Wantons, the Hunters and the Robinsons lived here. Should it be possible to go back in time, these past residents would immediately recognize their former homes. They would be able to walk again to the churches where they worshipped, to visit again the Redwood Library, to see once more the old State House, the Brick Market, and the Parade, as Washington Square was then called. Time has passed but little has changed. In the Point the past has been preserved in the present.

The Rivera House
Courtesy of the Newport Historical Society

The Sarah Kendall House, 47 Washington Street

Moving houses is always an interesting sport in Newport. This game flourished in the 18th Century and continued until after the beginning of the 1900s. After that time, it slowed. In the mid 1950s, with the restoration of colonial homes, it once again became popular. Many residents can remember a house aboard a huge trailer being slowly moved down the narrow streets to a new location while telephone and electric wires were temporarily removed to allow for its passage. The Point especially had the masters of the game. Sarah Kendall was the grand master.

A most unusual lady, she may never have moved mountains but she was an expert at moving houses. The block bounded by Washington, Poplar, Second and Elm Streets was her game board and she played Chinese checkers with most of the houses on that block.

Widow of Isaac Kendall, a New York merchant and philanthropist, she was one of the first persons known to move a house on the Point. She and her husband built a beautiful home on the corner of Washington and Elm Street. Many did not like the style of the high ceilings and French roof where most homes had a gable and gambrel style. Sarah always did her own thing.

She purchased almost all of the property east of her home that was on the south side of Elm Street. After that, she purchased all of the property on the east side of Washington Street from Poplar to Elm. She purchased the Miturn House, now demolished, and moved it to the east side of Washington Street and turned it sideways.

She purchased the Capt. Phillips House on the corner of Poplar and Washington Streets and moved it to the south side of Elm Street. She then moved a house from the south side of Elm Street to the lot where the Phillips house stood. Continuing her hobby, she then moved a small house from the south side of her home to the rear of the corner lot on Washington and Elm, later adding another building to it. She did not stop with these moves but continued on to Second Street where she realigned the neighborhood there. Sarah had an of idea of creating a neighborhood of fashionable boarding houses where the area already possessed many. Most of the residents did not object. One even stayed in her house cooking while it was being moved. Back then, one did not cook by electricity and the coal-stove heat was uninterrupted.

The Kendall house, as did many others, fell into disrepair during the war years. It was cut up and turned into apartments. The beautiful cupola on the top was removed. It was neglected and tenants moved in and out. No one seemed to care for this stately house.

On September 9, 1992, Bryan and Frances Babcock purchased the Kendall residence. With exquisite taste they remodeled it and restored it to its former eloquence, even to replacing the cupola that had once graced the building. It is now a bed and breakfast and a good-sized sign on the porch of the house bears Sarah's image. It is one of the most beautiful homes of the Point and Sarah would be proud if she could see it today.

The Faisneau House, 41 Washington Street

Etienne Pascal Faisneau came to Newport from France as a barber working for Count William Vernon. His home, the former Topham-Bigelow House, was at the time situated at the corner of Chestnut and Washington Street. He lived there until his death in 1845.

His granddaughter, Mrs. Batcheller added a wing with a large piazza to the old house, and it was then known as the Faisneau Boarding House. In 1885, there were about 75 lodging houses in Newport but they were disappearing. In 1914, the number had dwindled to 45 and in the 1950 there were few left. Today bed and breakfast inns have replaced them and as such are flourishing on the Point.

The Faisneau was a very popular boarding house. The porch, or piazza as they were then called, offered guests the opportunity to sit and enjoy the bay, the ships, and the shore. It is believed that the house was built prior to the Revolution.

After a long period of vacancy it was scheduled to be demolished in 1929. A colonial house and a small 19th Century house were part of the complex. The Oldport Association was formed in order to save these two buildings though the larger addition was demolished, the colonial and the little house were moved to the corner of Bridge and Washington Streets.

Oldport rented the houses for a period of time until William and Hazel Fullerton purchased and restored them. The little house is at the rear and is not easily viewed from the street. The Fullertons lived in the front house for many years. It stands today, looking as it did in colonial days, fully restored. It is now the home of Donald and Rowena Dery and overlooks Storer Park.

Home of the Pirate, Simeon Potter, 37 Marsh Street

Simeon Potter was born in Bristol, Rhode Island. He was not well educated and he had no love for King George II. When the King was at war with France and Spain, he saw a chance to profit. At age 24 he held a captain's license, and he purchased a share in a Newport ship "The Prince Charles of Lorraine."

In other words, he became a pirate but they were called by the nicer name of "Privateers." They had permission to seize, subdue and loot vessels belonging to the kings of Spain and France. With his brother-in-law and a crew of 80, they set sail Sept 8, 1744 with provisions for a six-month long cruise.

October 29th found them in French Guiana, terrorizing the inhabitants. They pillaged the town and the church and held the missionary priest hostage. They took all the furniture, the sacred vessels of the church, and all the silver they could find. They removed the locks and hinges from the doors and burned the church and the village. Potter had the church silver stamped with his initials.

He continued privateering for three more years, acquiring more ships. Only 27, he never went to sea again. He did not give up his ships but had his brother-in-law command them. He amassed a fortune in sugar, coffee, indigo, ivory, and the slave trade.

Now we have Simeon Potter, the maritime trader and patriot. Half of the Rhode Island vessels were engaged in smuggling. This meant that with the arrival of the British vessel, "H.M.S. Gaspee," which would patrol Narragansett Bay, every vessel would be in danger. The commander of the Gaspee had boasted time and again that he would seize the smugglers and treat them for what they were, "pirates."

John Brown, a prosperous merchant, was the leader of the colonists who opposed taxation without representation. There was no place in North America where men hated the King's method of seeking revenue more than here. Simeon Potter joined John Brown and they and the others planned to lure the Gaspee into shallow waters, then board and burn it.

The Gaspee spotted Brown's boat and pursued it. The Gaspee foundered in the shallow water and it ran aground. Brown, Potter and the others boarded it, captured and burned it to the water's edge while crowds on the shore near Bristol and Providence cheered. In 1775, Potter helped negotiate the end of the Bristol siege, but later British soldiers burned his home and those of 31 others.

There was another story about Simeon. He invested his spoils in shipping and real estate, owned eleven slaves and was the wealthiest man in Bristol. However, he was involved in many lawsuits. The most notorious of which was an attack on the Reverend Usher, 73 years of age, and the pastor of St. Michael's church. It seems that the minister admonished him from the pulpit. Simeon later accosted him and struck him, causing much injury. After the lawsuit which followed, and which Simeon lost, he moved to Swansea until public sentiment died down.

He became a philanthropist after the war. He donated this house, his former home in Newport, to the city to be used as a school for poor children. Jacob Dehane built the house in 1724.

The proprietors of Long Wharf opened the first Free School in this building at the corner of Washington and Marsh Streets in 1814. It had at times fifty pupils and operated until 1834 when it was deemed no longer necessary. The building was sold and the proceeds invested until a new school could be built.

In 1882, the new school was built on Elm Street and named Potter School. Although the building still stands, it too has outlived its usefulness as a school and is no longer used for that purpose. This is possibly the only school ever named for a pirate.

The Sarina Salvo Trust now owns the Simeon Potter house.

The Dinner Train, America's Cup Avenue

While the Old Fall River Line operated between Newport and New York, passenger trains carried people from Newport to Providence. However, when the Fall River Line ceased to exist and the steamers "Priscilla" and "Plymouth" were sold, the trains were no longer needed.

Many years ago, the Island Cemetery owned a little parcel of land on the corner of Burnside Avenue and Warner Street. Here they stored all the equipment necessary to maintain the cemetery grounds that were across the street. In 1915, having acquired a horse and wagon, they were now in need of shelter for the animal. In due course, a red brick building was built to house the animal and equipment.

However, the Cottrell family, who for three generations operated a very successful monument business, owned the adjoining land. Here they had a very small but charming house for their office. This little house was found to encroach on the land where the new stable was to be built. The Cottrells were asked to move the house within their own property line, which they did.

As the years passed, the Cottrells decided to sell their property. Douglas O'Neill purchased it for the site of his D&D Fencing Company. The little house was not needed and it was decided to demolish it.

Mrs. Edward Smith (Christy) looked at it, wanted it, and purchased it with the stipulation that it must be moved. By chance, her husband had a partner who was very much interested in the restoration of the Point. Tom Benson was born on the Point, a son of John Howard and Esther Fisher Benson. He had done so much to begin the restoration here. Certainly they had found the right man to help in the project.

One of the original members of "Oldport,", Tom was a graduate of Marlboro College where he majored in American Studies. Added to that, he owned 18 Elm Street and had land in the back. The little house was moved to this location with Tom taking a very active part in the moving process.

There it stood until Colonel Long took an interest and brought back the trains to Newport, not as a transportation service but as a tourist attraction. George King of New Hampshire, who had a long association with railroads, moved to Newport and together they smoothed the way for the delightful "Dinner Train" which Newport today enjoys.

What better spot for the little house to once again become an office. So it was moved once more. This time just a short distance where today it is part and parcel of Newport's Tourist Center.

Sadly, Tom left us at a very early age, but the little station is somewhat like a memorial to his memory and his dedication to the restoration of fine old homes. His ready smile is missed but his enthusiasm and charm will long be remembered.

The Howland House, 6 Bridge Street

Standing at the top of Bridge Street, near Thames Street, is a small saltbox house. Built in 1725 in South Dartmouth, Massachusetts, it was the farmhouse of Henry Howland and part of the Colonel Green Estate. Colonel Green was a descendent of Hetty Green, the famous "Witch of Wall Street."

Hetty Green started accumulating money in 1865 when her father left her a million dollars and a life interest in five million more. Shortly after an aunt left her a million more. In 1867, she married Edward Green, a millionaire in his own right, and by 1885 she had 26 million dollars. Edward Green lost his money and Hetty quickly lost him. She was an eccentric who lived under an assumed name in different boarding houses to avoid the tax assessor and save money. She would not part with a penny, and if she had to spend five cents, she demanded a receipt.

When her son Edward was a young boy, he injured his leg. She took him to a doctor under an assumed name and then refused to pay the bill. The doctor, upon discovering who she was, would no longer treat the young man until the bill was paid. Therefore young Edward did not receive the proper treatment and eventually had to have the leg amputated.

Dressed in black, she could be seen walking down the street to the Chemical National Bank in New York City where she was known. She would go to her vault, then sit cross-legged on the floor going through her stocks and bonds. She would not stop for lunch but would pull out an unwrapped ham sandwich from the folds of a garment that had many deep pockets. Sometimes she had over $200,000 in negotiable bonds in these pockets. Underneath her garments she stuffed old newspapers to keep her warm. Around her waist was a chain that carried keys to safe deposit boxes all over the country.

When she died in 1916, she left her son and daughter an estate worth over one hundred million dollars.

This little home was one of three buildings joined together on the former Green estate. It was the home of Henry Howland. It was almost 300 years old and owned by a religious group who were going to tear it down.

An early 18th century building, it had its original fireplace. The Newport Restoration Foundation purchased it in 1968. Pictures were taken before it was dismantled. The beams and boards were carefully measured and indexed and it was then moved, piece-by-piece, to Newport where it was stored in a warehouse until a site could be prepared for its reconstruction.

Restored, it is rented to carefully screened tenants who agree to open it to the public once a year, if the Foundation so desires.

Hetty Green

William Claggett House, 16 Bridge Street

William Claggett, the mechanical genius responsible for building the renowned Claggett clocks and organs was born in Wales in 1696. At age 12, he journeyed to Boston with his father, his brother Caleb and other family members. There he received a schooling that was not available to many children in the 16th century. Here he learned the skills of reading, writing and arithmetic.

It is believed that he was apprenticed to Benjamin Bagnall of Boston where he learned the skills that made him one of the most noted clockmakers of his day. His clocks are museum pieces and are as famous as the furniture of Townsend and Goddard.

At the age of 19, William married Mary Armstrong. A year later his first child, William, was born. In 1725, he purchased land on Bridge Street where he built his home. He leased the adjoining lot to his father, Caleb, who then built his stone-end home there. William and his family lived at 16 Bridge and his father and mother resided at 22 Bridge Street.

After his wife Mary Armstrong died, he married Rebecca Clarke. William fathered nine children, three of whom died in infancy. William died in Newport in 1749 at age 53 and was buried on Prescott Farm, Portsmouth, RI, near the road on the left hand side of the brook.

His will, dated July 13, 1748, left everything to his wife until his son Caleb reached 21. He gave small amounts of money to his son William and to his daughters Mary, Hannah and Elizabeth. There was no mention of a son named Thomas, who evidently was the last of the Claggett clockmakers. This does not mean that he disinherited Tom. Only the first page of the will is in the Newport Historical Society.

The rest of the will is missing. When the British evacuated Newport, a small vessel that accompanied the fleet, carried away many of the old records. This vessel was wrecked and the records waterlogged. When they were returned years later, many of them were ruined or incomplete.

William left all of his real estate, together with the rents of his shop standing on land belonging to the proprietors of Long Wharf in Newport, to his wife Rebecca until his son Caleb reached the age of 21. When Caleb reached that age, he would then equally share the rents and the profits of his real estate with his mother while she remained a widow.

William was everything from a clock and watchmaker to an organ builder, a compass maker, an engraver and printer, lecturer, author, notary public and experimenter in electricity. Some of the finest clocks made in New England during the 18th century were from the shop of William Claggett. One of his masterpieces now belongs to the Redwood Library.

His work was exceptional and a Claggett clock was a cherished item and bore his signature. People who owned these clocks treasured them. He made the original tower clock at Trinity church.

There are many stories about the Claggett clocks. One such story tells of a Claggett clock being transferred from one home to the new owner's home. Two men at opposite ends were carrying it with such solemnity that a passerby mistook the case of the clock for a coffin. He respectfully removed his hat and held his hand over his heart while the clock passed.

Another clock has stood, and still stands, in the very house where the owner placed it in 1740. Another, in the Sabbatarian Meeting House, has been there for more than two centuries and is still ticking.

When William Tilley, a Newport rope-maker wrote his will, he stipulated that his Claggett clock be bequeathed to the Tilley of each generation who bore the name George. The family complied with his wishes down to the 20th Century, when there was no heir of that name.

When a certain Loyalist family of pre-Revolutionary Newport fled to Canada, his Claggett clock went with him.

A joke that lives on in Newport is the story of the man who was having his grandfather clock repaired and serviced. Since he had no transportation, he carried it on a sling tied onto his back. A neighbor passing by taunted him, "Why don't you get a wristwatch like the rest of us?"

Thomas, his unmarried son, carried on his father's business. However, he evidently did not fare too well since John Townsend in 1783 forced Tom to sell his shop over a $149 debt. Evidently it was for cabinets built by John for Claggett clocks.

In another incident, Elizabeth Carey of Connecticut sued Tom. It concerned a lot of land that was situated on The Parade that is now Washington Square. Eventually this lot passed out of Claggett's hands and into the hands of John Townsend, cabinetmaker, who bought it for taxes.

In the year 1797, Tom Claggett was found in a nude state in Dyre's Swamp. That same year Job Townsend presented a bill for $2.00 for a coffin for Thomas Claggett to be paid out of the "Poor Fund." It appears that John Townsend and Tom Claggett did not have the friendliest business relationship.

It is amazing to think that these men created these beautiful clocks in a time when neither the tools nor the technology available today existed. More amazing is the fact that though these clocks still tick, the men whose knowledge and expertise produced them have been dead for over 200 years.

This illustrious home is the residence of James and Jessica Hagen.

Clocks - Mechanical and Biological

While writing about William Claggett, I thought, "What a strange invention the clock is?" It consists of a collection of cogs and gears that are always in motion. So many tiny pieces in a little miniature world where all parts move according to a function and each little part has a place.

The first mechanical clock was invented in the year 979 A.D., in Kaifeng, China. A young emperor commissioned it for the purpose of astrological fortune telling. It took eight years to construct and weighed more than two tons.

Even though it was of monstrous dimensions, it was remarkably efficient, striking a gong every 14 minutes and 22 seconds. At the same time, it turned the massive rings that were used to replicate the celestial movements of the sun, the moon and selected stars, all of which were crucial to Chinese astrological divination.

When the Tartars invaded China in 1108 they plundered the capital city and after disassembling the massive clock, carried it back to their own lands. Frustrated by their inability to put the precision piece back together, they melted it down for swords.

How essential is the mechanical clock? Could we survive without it? Man managed long before the first clock was invented for within each one of us there is another clock, the biological clock. This along with the mechanical clock governs our daily life, when we awake and when we sleep. The sun is also a clock. In any particular locale on any particular day, the time of sunrise is essentially the same from year to year. Man tells time by the clock and the calendar but how do the animals know? They, too, have a biological clock, an internal mechanism allowing them to tell time in order to survive.

On March 19th, within a 24-hour time frame of their predestined time, the swallows regularly return to Capistrano. Yearly, on October 15th, Monarch butterflies arrive from all parts and gather in the trees of Monterey, California. The variations of the weather and the availability of food do not seem to deter their arrival.

Yearly the North American bears hibernate. When the weather begins to turn cold, the bear begins to lower his body temperature. He also stores body fat, so that during the cold winter months he does not need to forage for food when it is scarce. The female mates before hibernation ensuring that the cubs will have ample time for nurturing in the spring.

The sparrows fly south and the squirrels gather their nuts in preparation for winter. Salmon, born in a river, spend their life in the sea. Instinctively twice a year, in spring and fall, battling the currents they return to the same waters where they were hatched. Here they spawn and die, thus ensuring the continuation of the species.

As complex and bewildering as the gears of the manmade clock were to the Tartars, nothing compares to the intricacy of the miracle of life created by God. One difference remains. While some mechanical clocks are still operating in perfect precision after 250 years, the biological clock of life stops much earlier.

Caleb Claggett House, 22 Bridge Street

Sometimes while doing the research for this book, I began to think that there were more Claggetts than there were Claggett clocks. Caleb Claggett, along with his other children, had a son William. He was the genius who built organs, experimented with electricity, and made clocks that are priceless museum pieces today. Then this William, among his nine children had a son Caleb and another son William and so on down the line until at times the generations blurred into one another.

Caleb Claggett, a Welshman and a baker married to Ann, came to Newport from Bristol, R.I. in 1717. With him came his family including his son William, the renowned clockmaker, who had been born in Wales in 1696. At this time William would have been twenty-one years of age.

The father and son lived in houses next to each other. The son William owned the land and he leased one of the parcels to his father. Caleb's house reflected his occupation. The lease, dated March 25, 1725, was for 25 years. It stipulated that within that time, a house 36 x 18, a bake house 20 x 40 with two large ovens, and a large wharf be built. This was done in less than three years. The house, bakeshop and wharf were completed before August 16, 1727. On that day, Caleb died at the age of 57 and was buried under a John Stevens' headstone in the Common Burying Ground.

The house was built in 1725. It had a central chimney and one brick end wall. Although brick was used for chimneys at the time, its use for an end wall without a chimney was very unusual and costly. The central chimney served four original rooms of the house. There is a question as to whether or not there was a four-room structure on this lot when Caleb leased it. These four rooms appear to be very old and very much like the houses that were built a century earlier in the 1600s. According to records

114

at that time, when William purchased the two lots, one of them contained a building.

At that time Bridge Street was known as Shipwright Street and ran along the edge of a cove. Originally the home was located wharf side, perhaps to allow a ship to load up on baked goods before setting off to sea.

Sometime after Caleb's death, the house was converted to a two family residence and over the years became seriously dilapidated. In the 1950s, the ridgepole was in such a deteriorated condition that this wonderful old house would possibly have fallen down within a year. The owners of the house received permission from the city to raze the building and put up a parking lot. Fortunately, Restorations, Inc. stepped in and saved this historic property from demolition. Further restoration took place under the ownership of Esther Morton Bates, a descendent of Quaker Tom Robinson. She purchased the house in 1956 and spent three years restoring it.

In the ensuing years it has been the home to many families. In the 1990s alone, it changed hands four times. Finally in July 1998, it was sold to Lisa and Bartlett Dunbar and has been lovingly restored. Mr. Dunbar also owned and restored 16 Bridge Street, the home of Caleb's son William. The restoration of these two houses helped increase the value of and the desire to own a house on the Point.

Home of the Unfortunate Hannah Robinson, 25 Bridge Street

A house was standing on this lot in 1727, when it was purchased by Peleg Carr from the estate of Edward Thurston. Carr's heirs indentured the property to Peter Simon in 1736. In the mid 1700s, Simon enlarged it. After the Revolution, Joshua Hammond purchased the house and it remained in the Hammond family until 1900. The house was restored through Operation Clapboard and is a private residence today. It will, however, always be remembered as the home of the unfortunate Hannah Robinson.

Hannah was a society beauty who lived in the mid-18th Century. She and her family lived in neighboring Narragansett. She was known for her unsurpassed beauty. Unfortunately, Hannah fell in love with her dance master, Peter Simon, Jr. Her father was enraged and violently opposed the match because of her tutor's low social position. However, Hannah eloped with him. The marriage occurred about 1760 or shortly thereafter. The ceremony was private and her father never knew who performed it.

She went with her husband to Providence where she exchanged the comfort of her father's home for a home of poverty. Her father disinherited her. Her husband was a gambler and his dissipated habits and neglect affected her health. She became languid and sickly. Peter brought her back to Newport where he finally deserted her.

Her father was a very wealthy man, known for his great hospitality. He numbered among his friends the elite of the colonies and of Europe. A noble, generous man by nature, he was easily aroused to anger, but was not vindictive and was forgiving and kind.

When he heard of Hannah's illness, he immediately went to her home taking some servants with him. On seeing him, Hannah threw her arms around him and he saw to it that she was placed on a litter and carried back to his home. At her request, they placed her down before the house and she exclaimed, "How beautiful it is." She died that night, but before she died, she requested that her father treat her husband kindly for her sake.

Peter Simon was at her funeral and stayed at her father's home for a short while. The family vault was not complete when Hannah died. About a month after the funeral, the vault was finished and her remains were transferred to the vault. Peter Simon went to France and never returned.

Rowland Robinson appears to have paid a heavy price for his disapproval of his daughter's marriage. In his old age he found himself alone. His two daughters were long since dead and his son died before his father, in Newport around 1804, without children.

He was a lonely old man and had neither the spirit nor the inclination to make a will. His large estate was, upon his death, divided by law among his brothers and sisters and their heirs.

Now we run into a little bit of a mystery. According to most accounts, Hannah died without issue. However, research shows there is more to this story.

Dr. William Bowen of Providence frequently visited Rowland Robinson's house. There is reason to believe that these two families were very friendly. Benjamin Bowen, who was a cousin of Dr. Bowen, died February 21, 1784 at age 57. In his will, he left to young Hannah the furniture that came into his hands from her mother Hannah Robinson Simon.

In the book "Old Families of R.I." it is recorded that Hannah Robinson Simon, daughter of Hannah Simon, became the bride of Dr. Joseph Bowen, son of Benjamin Bowen. So it appears that Hannah's daughter married Benjamin Bowen's son Joseph. Further records in Gloucester, RI, show that Dr. Joseph Bowen had a son Clovis who was the father of Hannah Robinson Bowen born April 16, 1841, Hannah Simon Bowen born August 7, 1857, and Herbert Robinson Bowen born August 25, 1861.

There are now unanswered questions. If it is true that Hannah had a daughter, why was Hannah's father alone in his final years? Why did his assets and land go to his brothers and sisters instead of to his granddaughter? How did Hannah Robinson Simon's furniture come into the possession of Benjamin Bowen? Perhaps the daughter was a minor and Benjamin Bowen, given the closeness of the families, became young Hannah's guardian. It seems evident that she married his son, Joseph, and that together they had a son, Clovis who was the father of two daughters and a son.

The resultant generations were:

    (1) Hannah Robinson Simon ....mother

    (2) Hannah Simon Bowen ....daughter

    (3) Clovis Bowen ....grandson

    (4) Hannah Robinson Bowen....great granddaughter,

          Hannah Simon Bowen ....great granddaughter and

          Herbert Robinson Bowen....great grandson.

If the records are true, then the first Hannah Robinson was certainly unfortunate but forgotten she never has been.

In the early 1950s, the Newport National Bank, formerly the Rivera House, was remodeled. An ell was added in such a way as not to destroy the original configuration of the building. The wainscoting, panels, post and other architectural details were copied from the Peter Simon house. It is one of Newport's many important examples of the same period as the Rivera House, making it one of the many outstanding 18th Century buildings still standing in the Newport.

Dr. Abiel (Abel) Spencer, 43 Bridge Street
(House is no longer standing.)

Dr. Abiel Spencer was born in East Greenwich, RI and came to Newport in his early years. He was a cabinetmaker who learned his trade as an apprentice of John Goddard. Probably no man lived so methodical a life as Dr. Spencer (for so he was called). He had a tiny shop on the Point where he lived in a little world of his own, undisturbed by what was going on in the world around him.

In 1810, he bought the place. Except for about 10 years, when he was in charge of a woolen mill in Portsmouth, he passed his whole life under this roof, dying in 1878 at an advanced age. For 68 years he had this little shop. So averse was he to leaving it, that he rarely went as far as Thames Street, not much more than once in ten years. It is only two blocks away.

At first he kept a few groceries. He added medicine to his stock and became a dispenser of the most popular remedies. The city census listed him as a saw filer and druggist. The shop was scarcely ten by twelve feet. One wondered how he could move about it without disturbing the little bottles and notions that were in every corner and crevice. On one side of the shop there was a lean-to, even smaller than the shop, in which he did a little jobbing. He could fix anything. He could file a saw, make a mouse-trap, or spread plaster. One day he would make a wooden claw foot for a pedestal, and the next day he would restore the wind to a broken bellow.

He always wore a hat and was never without it. He put it on when he rose in the morning. The last thing at night, before blowing out the candle, he would remove it from his head and place it by his bed-side. Indoors and outdoors, it was the same. When he sat down to his meals, his hat was always on his head. One reason he gave for not going to a meeting was that he would have to remove his hat. Although he rarely left the neighborhood, he knew what was going on in the world. He loved reading, conversed well, and had a retentive memory. Many people found it pleasant to go to his little shop and have long talks with him.

So he passed his days. After sixty-eight years of selling drugs behind the little counter, his own light grew dim, his glasses were laid aside, and the hat that had almost become a part of him rested undisturbed by his bedside. He died February 1878, aged 90 years, one month and four days.

The Sherman Clarke House, 67 Bridge Street

This stately house was built in 1749. It stands on land that once belonged to Michael and John Hattub, owners of the American Ice and Coal Company. Michael and his family resided in a cottage on the corner that is now a lovely garden. In the ensuing years, the coal and ice company went out of business and the house burned down leaving only the foundation. The then young John Hattub operated a drive-in liquor store where the coal company had been. Eventually this also closed and Nathaniel Norris purchased the property.

In the early 1970s, the face of Newport was changing dramatically. Houses were being demolished in the downtown area to make way for America's Cup Avenue.

At 279 Thames Street, opposite the present post office, stood the pre-revolutionary home of Sherman Clarke. Along with other buildings in this area, many very impressive, this lovely home was slated to be demolished. Nathaniel Norris had the foresight to purchase this house, intending to move it to his Bridge Street location.

As with many of the historic homes in Newport, the history of the house is unique. Sherman Clarke owned the house but Thomas Banister owned the land. Mr. Banister being a Tory had his land confiscated and thus Sherman Clarke lost his house. In time, the seized property was sold to Aaron Sheffield. Later Benjamin Mumford, who held the political appointment of postmaster in Newport in 1813, purchased it. He then moved the post office into this building using the rear quarters as his residence.

In 1887, Simeon Davis purchased the building and converted the west side into the Davis Bakery.

Many other commercial enterprises followed. Eventually it became a boarding house. One of the lodgers, a bookie who at this time was being held at the Adult Correctional Institution, evidently fearing that unwanted evidence in his room might be discovered and used to convict him, hired one of his employees to set the house on fire.

Fortunately the blaze was extinguished and the building saved. In February 1873 the house was moved to its present site. Restoration followed and most of the house is still original, including the bull's-eye glass in the transom over the front door, the door itself, the wide-plank floors, the fireplaces and the posts and beams. Some of these show evidence of the bookie's blaze. No one was ever apprehended for the attempted arson.

The next owners, Roger and Katherine Kirby, further renovated the home by converting the unfinished attic into a full third floor.

It is now the home of Mr. and Mrs. Albert Lowe who love it, and feel that they are the caretakers of this lovely house that has sheltered so many different personalities: a Tory, a bookie, a postmaster, a baker and countless unknown others.

The John Townsend House, 70 Bridge Street

John Townsend, son of Christopher and Patience Easton Townsend, was born in 1732. He became the best known of the entire clan. He bears the distinction of being one of America's finest furniture makers. John probably trained in his father's shop. The craft was perpetuated in the family for as many as four or five generations. It is not known whether or not slaves were employed in the furniture making part of the business. It is known that John Townsend owned three slaves and they very well could have been using their woodworking skills learned in the West Indies or West Africa.

The Townsends owned many houses on the Point. Business thrived until the Revolution when Quakers were persecuted for their anti-war sentiments. John was a Quaker and attended silent meetings at least twice a week.

In 1767, John married Philadelphia Feke, daughter of the artist Robert Feke. They had five children: Sarah, Solomon, Mary, John F. and Charles F. Townsend. John was suspected of being a spy during the Revolutionary War. He was taken prisoner in October 1777 and put aboard the British ship Lord Sandwich in Newport Harbor. He was released a few weeks later when Governor Cooke arrived and an exchange of prisoners between the British and the colonials was made. It is possible that at that time he moved to Connecticut to join his wife's family who had settled there. The British left Newport in 1779. How soon he returned to Newport after that is not known.

Due to the British occupation and the blockade of the port, furniture making was minimal. Only mending and maintenance was required. The French, when they arrived, were friendly and always paid for their purchases in cash but times were hard. The distressing conditions of the town following the war were evident on June 27, 1783. On that day, the shop of Tom Claggett was sold at public auction for $149.00 for the satisfaction of John Townsend of Newport. A bill probably due for clock cases. Little is known of Tom's activities after that.

In 1792, John labored in his Newport shop to complete a chest. Two centuries later this chest caused a bidding war that brought 4.73 million dollars. This was the third highest price paid at auction for any piece of furniture. In 1800, when he was 67 years of age, John Townsend produced the last documented work of his career. He died at age 76, six years after the death of his wife.

Mary was evidently her father's favorite for in his will he left her the bulk of his possessions. It is believed that many of these pieces were built in anticipation of John's marriage. There is also the possibility that many came to John from his father Christopher.

Forty-seven years later, Mary passed on leaving most of her possessions, which included her father's legacy, to her nephew Christopher Townsend, son of her brother John F. Townsend. In 1881, Christopher left all of it to his sister Ellen who never married and died five years after and she had no near relatives. In her will, she left a sum of money, all her household furnishings and a rich endowment of Newport furniture to her executor, John S. Coggeshall, to be distributed "as if she were alive."

No records survive of how Ellen's executors disposed of her furniture. William Sheffield and his sister were both mentioned in her will. Today the Sheffield family owns a number of handsome articles of Townsend furniture that may represent posthumous gifts from the elderly lady. They may also have been acquired from her estate by purchase.

The east portion of this home originally stood on Marsh Street. It was moved and placed on this site beside the original Townsend house and beautifully renovated by Mrs. Henrietta Dane. A house that stood on the West side was demolished leaving room for a garden and shed.

The Christopher Townsend House, 74 Bridge Street

In 1640, three Townsend brothers, Henry, John and Richard, left England and settled in an early Quaker community in Warwick, RI. Finally after three moves, they settled in Long Island, N.Y.

In 1807, John's grandson Solomon received permission to leave and join the Quaker community in Newport. Here he brought his four children Job, Christopher, Solomon and Hannah. Solomon Sr. died nine years later. Young Solomon became a seafarer and Hannah married John Goddard.

Christopher was born in 1701, two years after his brother Job. The brothers considered themselves house or ship carpenters as well as furniture makers. Christopher served time at sea. In 1718, he was aboard the "Elizabeth" when pirates overtook it.

In 1723, Christopher married Patience Easton, daughter of Nicholas Easton, one of the first settlers of the island whose descendants sold the grant known as Easton's Point to the Quaker church for settlement. He and Job were among the first Quakers to buy lots here. About 1725, Christopher built his home at 74 Bridge Street when he was only 24 years of age. He later added the shop to it. He and Patience had four children: John, Jonathan, Christopher, Jr. and Mary. Jonathan died in 1772 at the age of 27.

Christopher was the most prosperous of his relatives. He acquired most of his wealth specializing in desks both for export and local use. A secretary bookcase created by him in 1745 fetched 8.25 million dollars at a Sotheby's auction a few years ago. The desk was discovered in France. The piece was made for the Rev. Nathaniel Appleton, minister of the First Church in Cambridge, Massachusetts in the 1700s. A descendant of Appleton's who served in the diplomatic corps emigrated to France in the

1800s and it is believed that he took the desk with him.

In 1773, Christopher died leaving to his children John, Christopher Jr., and Mary one third each interest in his entire inventory that was for sale, except for one mahogany desk that his son Jonathan (deceased in 1772) had made. This desk he left to Christopher, Jr. He left all his tools to John.

Like the Goddard family, the Townsends were a large extended Quaker family. They not only worked together with the Goddards, they intermarried with them. The Goddards and the Townsends were the dominant force in the furniture industry. Together these two families, unexcelled craftsmen, produced furniture of such superb quality that it became known throughout the colonies. Today, their workmanship is displayed in museums throughout the world.

This is now the home of Mr. and Mrs. Robert Goddard.

The Pineapple House, 36 Walnut Street

This adorable little one-story gambrel roof house sits on the southwestern corner of Second and Walnut Streets. It bears a pineapple, which in colonial days was used for decoration. They were mainly placed outside the homes over doorways and even on the roofs. When the seafarer returned after a long absence, he would spend the first few days with his family and then place a pineapple over the doorway. His friends would then know that they were welcome to visit and share the tales of his voyage. Pineapples were then, and today still are, considered the symbol of hospitality.

Known throughout the Point, this house was built somewhere after 1740. It experienced the violence of the Revolution when the British occupied Newport. Almost two hundred years later, it witnessed the brutal murder of Miss Susan Franklin, a beloved Newport teacher, on April 23, 1953.

The first owner we are aware of was Joseph Betcher, a pewterer whose work was well known. After the Revolution, a Mr. Edward Watson purchased it and it remained in his family until 1907. In the 1930s a Mr. Arthur Leslie Green purchased it but never lived in it. However, he had a post mounted on the corner of the house with a carved pineapple. This was about 1930. The pineapple is still there today. A very fancy "S" is bolted on the chimney.

Mr. Greene turned the house into a museum of antiques. He opened the house only by appointment, charged a fee and gave the money to charity. This was not the only house owned by Mr. Greene. He was also the owner of the Weaver-Franklin House that he had moved from the corner of Second and Walnut to Training Station Road. There he constructed a second house that he called the Cranford Cottage.

The pineapple sitting on top of the post on the corner denotes a welcome to all. The house has changed hands numerous times since Miss Franklin resided there but it will always be remembered as her home. It is a tiny home full of memories.

This house is now the home of Alfred and Marion Lowe.

Matthew Calbraith Perry House, 31 Walnut Street

Diagonally across the street from the Pineapple House, on the northeast corner of Walnut and Second Street is the home that was the birthplace of Commodore Matthew Calbraith Perry, brother of Commodore Oliver Hazard Perry.

Calbraith was one of the five sons and three daughters of Capt. Christopher Raymond Perry and his wife Sarah. Oliver Hazard Perry, the first born, and another brother and sister, Raymond and Sarah, were all born in Narragansett R.I., on land owned by the Perry family since 1703.

They were the great grandchildren of Edward Perry, a peaceful Quaker, who emigrated from England and settled on the Cape in Massachusetts. Edward's son, Freeman, left Massachusetts and settled in Wickford, marrying Mary Hazard. He practiced medicine and was appointed Chief Justice of the Court and was known as Judge Perry. It was his son, Christopher, who was the father of Matthew and Oliver.

The Perrys were peaceful Quakers, and it was Christopher who was the first to break from this Quaker tradition of his forebears. At age 14 or 15, against the wishes of his father, Judge Perry, he joined a militia company called the "Kingston Reds." Christopher, fully dedicated to the American cause, killed one of his father's neighbors, a Quaker farmer, Simeon Tucker, in 1777. Tucker, consistent with his religion, made no secret of his beliefs and refused to pay taxes or give food and blankets to the Continental Army. The Kingston Reds decided to teach him a lesson. A squad under Colonel Maxon marched to his home. The farmer was dragged outside.

Colonel Maxon, who was in charge, ordered his men to level their muskets and once again requested the Quaker farmer to obey. The farmer again refused. Some claimed that the Colonel instructed his men to fire over the farmer's head and that Perry did not hear this. A bullet from the musket of Christopher Perry, not yet 16, pierced the farmer's heart. All others missed. The farmer's body was then dragged into the house and thrown at Mrs. Tucker's feet.

After the killing of Simeon Tucker, Christopher was not eager to remain in his native town and he went to Boston and signed on a privateering vessel. His war record was colorful. He saw service on land and sea during the Revolutionary War and four times was taken prisoner by the British. During his confinement in Ireland, he met Sarah Wallace Alexander, a blue eyed Irish beauty, whom he vowed he would make his wife. In 1761, she accompanied him to America where they were soon married in his father's home where father and son were reunited after seven years.

Judge Perry gave his son Christopher ten acres of land where he maintained a hunting and shooting lodge in Matunuck. So it was here in South County where the three oldest children were born. However, Captain Christopher decided to move to Newport where he leased a home on "The Point." His father purchased it and would, in 1800, deed it to Christopher. Capt. Perry settled in Newport and invested his money in ships and cargoes and increased his fortune before misfortune and the depression hit.

The Point was the aristocratic section of Newport in the 18th century. It was here in this cozy gambrel house that young Matthew Calbraith Perry, the couple's fourth child, was born on April 10, 1781. Matthew was given the middle name of Calbraith after a fellow Irish passenger on his parent's voyage to America. He was called "Cal" (pictured to the right).

Oliver and Calbraith grew up in an era of great prosperity. Newport was the most cosmopolitan town in the United States next to New York. Private schools were so good that many of the prominent left their children there year round. Oliver and Calbraith attended one of these schools.

Oliver, Cal and the other "Over to the Point" sons of gentlemen mixed with, played with, and fought with the sons of the laborers and stevedores who lived around lower Thames Street. However, with their family's wealth, they had good private schools. The Perry children attended Trinity Church. They had lots of open country nearby where they had picnics, shooting, skating and the bay where they fished and had sailing parties. It was a wonderful life for a boy.

Matthew Calbraith Perry
Courtesy of The Rhode Island
Historical Society

Calbraith and Oliver went on to a lifetime of adventure in the Navy. Both had their own commands. Oliver is best known as the hero of the Battle of Lake Erie. He traveled the world. In 1819, he contracted yellow fever off the Port of Spain Trinidad and died aboard his flagship the John Adams at the age of 34. Knowing that death was imminent Oliver made provisions that his wife would inherit all his possessions. Meanwhile, in Newport, Betsy had a dream that Oliver had died but stated that she was not superstitious and would not let it worry her. Not too long after, she received word that Oliver was dead.

The doctors recommended that the body be interred in Trinidad rather than risk the crew's exposure to infection by bringing the body back to the United States. On August 24, 1819, he was buried in Lapyrouse Cemetery in Trinidad with full military honors. The nation grieved and Congress made a liberal provision for his wife Betsy and his family. His mother, who depended upon him for support, was also granted a pension.

In 1826, his remains were brought back from Trinidad on the sloop of war "The Lexington," arriving on the 27th of November. Once again Oliver was buried, this time supposedly in Trinity Churchyard. He was later disinterred, when the State of Rhode Island erected a large granite monument in his memory on the west side of Island Cemetery and buried once more with full military honors. Oliver Hazard Perry was possibly the only man who was buried three times. Cal felt deeply the loss of the brother he dearly loved.

Calbraith is best remembered for his part in the surrender of Japan in 1854, whereby Japan agreed to open its ports to Western trade. In 1853, Cal was sent on a mission to Japan, a country that had been closed to outsiders since the 17th century. The United States Government, as a consequence of complaints made to it that American seamen, wrecked on the coast of Japan had been very harshly dealt with by the authorities of that country, sent Cal to demand protection for the American seamen. He was also to negotiate a treaty in which American vessels would be allowed to enter one or more ports to obtain supplies for the purpose of trade. Cal, with great skill and tact, succeeded and a treaty was signed on March 31, 1854, which opened the ports of Shimoda and Hakodate to United States commerce. This was one of the most important factors in determining American policy in Asia and was a remarkable feat. The effects of this treaty are still felt in America in the 21st Century. It also enabled Japan to develop into a modern nation.

After his return from Japan, Cal was not in good health. At age 63, Cal caught a severe cold and died in New York on March 4, 1858. He expressed a wish to be buried in Newport, but because of the severe weather, his body was placed in the burial vault of his wife's family in St. Mark's churchyard in New York. Eight years later the body was transferred to Newport, as he had wished. He was buried in the Island Cemetery near his parents and brother Oliver. Their lives took them to many distant parts of the world but it was to Newport that they wished to return.

Pictured on the next page is the gravesite of Oliver Hazard Perry located in the Island Cemetery. It holds some of the most beautiful examples of stone carving. It is amazing how few people know of the lives of the famous persons buried here and of the tremendous talent of the men who carved their monuments. The history within its boundaries is endless.

Oliver Hazard Perry's Gravesite

The "Standing Angel," pictured below, is a large statue by the Irish born sculptor Augustus Saint-Gaudens. It is one of the many outstanding memorials in the Island Cemetery. It stands on the Smith plot not very far from the graves of Oliver and Matthew Calbraith Perry.

Over the years, the house has seen many changes. A liquor/grocery store was put on the first floor. The house was not raised when the stores were built. Instead, an exterior stairway was added to give access to the upper stories.

Matthew Crilley, owner of the liquor store, was stabbed one night when he resisted a robbery attempt. Hospital Apprentice Benjamin Willis and Seaman Apprentice William Bradshaw, both 20 years of age, were arrested by Newport police on May 27, 1963, and charged with murder. Mr. Crilley died of his wounds at the Newport Hospital. They were sentenced to life imprisonment.

During the years that Doris Duke and the Newport Restoration Foundation were restoring the colonial homes, this home was fully restored to its original loveliness. The liquor and grocery store were removed and the house restored to its original design. The house then became the residence of George and Eleanor Weaver who lived in it while they were building a new home.

The Battle of Lake Erie

One of the great naval battles of the War of 1812 was fought not on the ocean but on the fresh water of the Great Lakes.

In 1813, the British held Canada and controlled Lake Erie. In the spring of that year, a twenty-eight year old naval officer was sent to Erie, Pennsylvania with orders to build a fleet of ten ships and lead it against the enemy. He was Commander Oliver Hazard Perry.

Perry was aboard "The Lawrence," named after his close friend James Lawrence who had been killed a few months earlier. Perry had a flag made up with the words: "Don't give Up The Ship," which were the dying words of Lawrence.

On September 10th, Perry met up with a British Squadron and opened fire. Soon "The Lawrence" was wrecked by British cannon balls. Taking his flag down, Perry transferred to another of his ships, "The Niagara."

Sailing though the enemy lines with cannon blasting, he bombarded the British for a full fifteen minutes. The British surrendered and Perry sent General William Harrison this famous message: "We have met the enemy and they are ours."

This victory gave the United States control of Lake Erie.

John Goddard House, 81 Second Street

The costliest American piece of furniture sold at auction for $11 million in 1989. It was a Newport desk by John Goddard who made the piece about 1767 for John Nicholas Brown.

John Goddard was born to Daniel and Mary Tripp Goddard on January 20, 1724. His father was listed as a shipwright, housewright and carpenter.

The first record of John is when he was made a free man on April 3, 1745. He did not own land at this time, but he was 21 and his father's oldest son. He was probably the most famous cabinetmaker that Newport ever produced and Newport produced many. John was a member of a whole clan of cabinet-makers. He worked as an apprentice to Job Townsend and he married Townsend's daughter Hannah in 1746. At least 20 craftsmen came from the Townsend-Goddard families.

John first purchased land in 1748 at the corner of Washington and Willow Streets. Here he built his house and a shop attached to the house but later this shop was detached. In 1868, the house was moved from the corner of Washington and Willow Streets to make way for the Villa Marina. The house was then moved to 81 Second Street. Goddard's workshop was moved to Smith Street off Poplar Street but that building was demolished in the late 1950s. A replica of the workshop was added to the back of the house in recent years. It serves as a guesthouse.

In 1774, there were apparently fifteen individuals in the Goddard household including seven under the age of 16. No black people were listed as living there but it is thought that his family, like the Townsends, did own slaves.

When he died in 1785, he left all his stock of mahogany to his sons to be "worked up" for the benefit of his wife and minor children. In 1786, the local newspaper carried an article advising creditors that John Goddard died insolvent and all claims against his estate should be sent to Townsend Goddard. The Revolutionary War had a disastrous effect on many Newport merchants.

At the time that the Goddard House was moved to this location, there were few houses in the area. Unfortunately over the years surrounding acreage was broken into small lots and sold. There were no zoning laws at that time to prevent overcrowding. For many years, the house was untenanted and fell into disrepair. The neighborhood deteriorated. It was rescued during the days of restoration in Newport and is once again a family residence. Mr. and Mrs. Albert Henry meticulously restored the house between 1968 and 1970. It is very likely, but not authenticated, that John himself carved the woodworking within the house.

John Goddard made buffets, tall clock cases, high backed chairs, card tables, and sideboards, all of superb workmanship. Goddard was a gifted craftsman. Although he became far more famous, he was not considered as gifted as his teacher, Job Townsend.

This house is now the home of Ian and Joy Scott.

13. Colonial Cemeteries, Farewell Street

One of the oldest Colonial cemeteries in America is the Coddington Cemetery that lies at the southern end of Farewell Street. It is a very small cemetery but within its boundaries lie the bodies of six Colonial Governors. Among them is Governor William Coddington, who died at the age of 77, and who in his will, bequeathed this land as a cemetery for Quakers. Governor Coddington had three wives and 13 children. He was buried in this plot of ground, now known as Coddington Cemetery, close to his Marlborough St. home. Three master stonecutters named Stevens carved many of the gravestones all of whom had the first name John.

There are many other colonial cemeteries throughout the city. We shall consider only those near the Point. In the Common Burial Ground on the northern end of Farewell Street, there is a treasury of colonial monuments divided into two sections. The south side was for the freemen and the north side for the slaves.

Although they bore the label of slaves, their Newport masters treated them rather kindly. Many slave owners were generous and liberal in their treatment of their slaves. They cared not only for their general prosperity, but arranged their marriages, assisted in their religious worship, and permitted them to accumulate private funds, often to buy their freedom. When they died many of them were buried in their owner's family plots. Nearly a thousand stones stand, dated between 1600 and 1800, examples of the finest sculpture. They include the works of John Stevens, whose shop is still in existence today. As the century proceeded, the stones became more elaborate. Each engraving was carved and signed by the artist.

Adjacent to this burial ground is the Island Cemetery with entrances both on Farewell and Warner Street. In this private cemetery are the monuments of Oliver Hazard Perry and Matthew Calbraith Perry, Newporters who lived in splendor and also died in splendor.

The Braman Cemetery and the City Cemetery are on the opposite side of Farewell Street. In the Braman Cemetery there is a section that is apportioned for Jews. Here the Jew and Gentile lie together. There is another Jewish cemetery at the top of Touro Street, in the section of Newport known as Historic Hill. This cemetery, which is described in Chapter 7, dates back to 1677.

Many people pass this cemetery and quietly glance behind the locked gates with never a thought for the Hebrews who lie beneath the shadow of a Cypress tree. These were people who gave so much to Newport, who loved the city and who chose it as their final resting place. No one has been buried in this cemetery for the past 150 years. Its gates are locked.

14. Other Homes on the Point

The Newport Historical Commission, that dictates how you may renovate or restore your home, governs the houses within the historic district of the Point. On the Point all the land that lies between Long Wharf and Van Zandt Avenue is considered to be in the historic district.

Many homes on the Point have stories that are unknown, for each house has its own secrets. Many homes were owned, many were rented, but people found shelter under their roofs. Some have sheltered five generations of the same family. Each home had someone who cared for it until it was time to leave, time to turn it over to someone else.

Whether they were tenements, cottages or small mansions, the houses tell us in their own way of the very different dreams of those who lived within their walls. They are memorials to those who struggled and to those who had power and wealth. Different as they may have been, the occupants and their dreams would one day leave only to be replaced by other occupants, other dreams.

The houses remain today as constant reminders of those who were here before us, those who led the way. Rational and unsentimental though you may be, you must admit that although the time and place will never be recaptured, these historic homes, built when America was young and proud, will continue to bring joy and beauty to all.

It would be impossible to illustrate all the lovely homes on the Point. The previous pages have displayed many historical homes. Others have been built in recent years and most of them have been designed to fit into the neighborhood. All have sheltered different people with different aspirations and different destinies.

Like the historic homes, they are lovely to look at. They are part of the Point, charming and picturesque. Although their stories have yet to be written, time will give them an identity of their own

Each represents the American dream.

*Chestnut Inn Bed & Breakfast
99 Third Street*

12 Battery Street

24 Van Zandt Avenue

10 Van Zandt Avenue

35 Second Street

103 Second Street

13 Bayside Avenue

9 Bayside Avenue

71 Washington Street

53 Washington Street

129 Washington Street

123 Washington Street

11 Pine Street

25 Walnut Steet

15. Stories

Since the beginning of mankind we have told stories. We have all listened to them, simple tales fashioned from the fabric of life and others spun from the world of our imagination. Yet, whether fact or fiction, these stories begin and have always begun with a special moment, an experience, a feeling, or a thought.

Whether a thousand years ago or today in our highly mechanized, computerized society, stories have been told for basically the same reasons. These reasons are to educate, to entertain, to explain, to honor the past and its people, and to record the simple and seemingly important and unimportant moments of human existence.

Throughout the entire world, in every culture, people have told stories at home, at work, when the crops were being harvested, when the fish were being caught, when the wood was being cut, when the wool was woven, when the women gathered, and when the men sought companionship, anywhere that there is a storyteller and a listener.

Today we still enjoy stories, listening to them, telling them, as deeply as our ancestors did, for our lives are bound together with stories. The tales, perhaps some very ordinary, that seem to catch us up and in some obscure, almost magical way, help us to make sense of our world.

We hope that the stories on the preceding pages have brought to the reader some enjoyable moments and perhaps some fond memories.

Finale

We have looked at Newport as it was over 200 years ago, as it was 50 years ago and as it is today. What will it be like 50 years from now? What changes will man have wrought?

This old part of Newport, the Point, the most conservative, will possibly not change at all. The Historic Preservation Society, as well as the Point Association, protects the area. The inhabitants who occupy the old wooden houses will continue to restore and preserve them. These houses will still stand on the edge of the sidewalk as they have always done. The narrow streets will remain the same. St. John's Church will still ring its bell. At Battery Park, the water will still wash over the rocks, the same fog will roll into the harbor, the fog horns will wail, the tide will rise and fall on the shore with the same rhythmical flow, the storms will still thunder, the sun will still set at eventide.

Within the Point itself there is neither a hotel nor a store and I know of no section of Newport where they are less wanted. There are, however, a large number of bed and breakfast accommodations.

Aquidneck Island means "Isle of Peace." The Point is the place where people who want to rest from their cares will find it. They can walk in peace, see the sun rise and set, look out onto the bay, smell the salt air and feel the wind on their face.

Goat Island as seen from Battery Park

Bibliography

Trial of Anne Hutchinson   Newport Historical Society

Home of Gov. Wm. Coddington   Newport Historical Society

Slavery   Coombs, Norman. *The Black Experience in America.* Twayne Press, 1972

Burning of of the Gaspee   Rhode Island Historical Society

Jewish Cemetery   Newport Daily News, 1999

Hanging of Mary Dyre   Newport Historical Society

Newport Torpedo Station   Newport Historical Society

Tax deeds and records of houses   Newport City Hall

Moving the Wissahickon   Newport Historical Society

Liturgical Art   Bethune, Ade. *EYE CONTACT WITH GOD THROUGH PICTURES*. Kansas City, MO: Sheed & Ward, 1986

Peter Quire   Newport Historical Society

Silhouette of Captain Parkin   *Now and Then on the Point*. Reprinted from THE GREEN LIGHT, Bulletin of the Point Association of Newport, 1980

Colonial couple   *Now and Then on the Point*. Reprinted from THE GREEN LIGHT, Bulletin of the Point Association of Newport, 1980

Rivera House   Newport Historical Society

Matthew Calbraith Perry   Rhode Island Historical Society, Newport Historical Society, Providence Journal

Townsend-Goddard Families   Newport Historical Society

Map of the Point

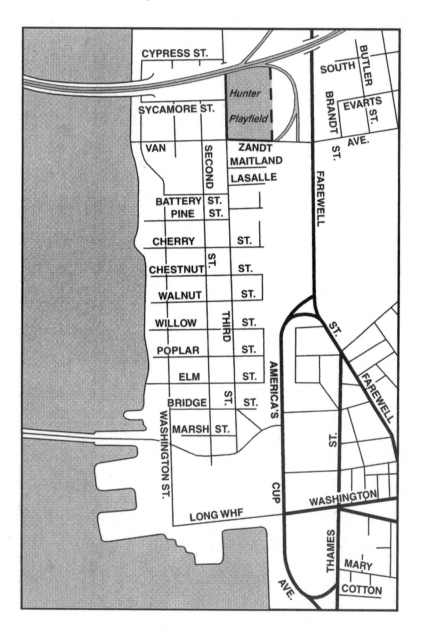